I0820420

ABOUT EXTRAORDINARY BOOKS

Extraordinary Books is a not-for-profit company bringing a new approach to publishing. We were founded with a sense of outrage at the ever-growing monopoly exerted by the big publishers, and a desire to subvert the current state of the industry.

Here's what that looks like:

- We're seeking authors with something unique to contribute – a book only they could have written. Whether an author has thousands of followers on social media, or has never heard those two words joined before, we're committed. No platform? No problem. We're not driven by market trends; we look for books that are one of a kind.
- All our books receive equal, substantial attention and marketing budgets, and we share profits with our authors 50/50. As for us? We only need enough to keep publishing without compromise.
- We're guided by curatorial openness: our experienced team commissions books in-house, and our visionary editorial collective helps uncover singular writing.

Whether speculative fiction, art, memoir or anything in between, our books have this in common: a distinctive pairing of author and subject.

If that means publishing niche books, so be it. If it means going beyond the constraints of genre, we're up for that. If it means taking risks, bring it on.

We're for readers. *Not for profit.*

Extraordinary Books
Gable House, 18–24 Turnham Green Terrace
London W4 1QP
www.extraordinarybooks.co.uk

Published in Great Britain in 2025 by Extraordinary Books

ISBN 978-1-917569-00-2
eISBN 978-1-917569-01-9

EU GPSR authorised representative: Logos Europe
9 rue Nicolas Poussin, 17000
La Rochelle, France.
contact@logoseurope.eu

Printed and bound in Great Britain by Clays Ltd, Elcograf S.p.a.

RUNNING AMOK

Inside the Mind of the Lone Mass Killer

PAUL E. MULLEN

EXTRAORDINARY
BOOKS

CONTENTS

Introduction

THIS BOOK IS about perpetrators of a form of murder unknown in Western nations until relatively recently. The emergence of the cultural script for lone mass killers is rooted in the profound changes undergone in our societies since the twentieth century, which have created individuals so alienated and disaffected that they choose to try and kill others and then themselves for the sake of their fifteen minutes of fame and a semblance of power and significance.

I have had more direct clinical experience than almost any other forensic psychiatrist of assessing and managing lone-actor perpetrators of massacres. However, my involvement began not in this capacity, but as a member of a New Zealand community that suffered such an attack. I lived with my family beside Dunedin Harbour, a few kilometres from the township of Aramoana – where a massacre that claimed the lives of fourteen people occurred on the evening of 13 November 1990.

We were at home when we were disturbed by the sound of gunfire. It was not the sound made by rifles used to shoot rabbits, with which we were familiar; this was the sound produced by the discharge of military weaponry. The initial outburst of shooting was followed by briefer episodes of firing throughout the evening and late into the night. Police, ambulances and – early the following morning – military forces drove past the end of our road on the way down harbourside. A phone call from a colleague at the hospital at about 9 PM gave me the first indication that the shooting was coming from Aramoana.

A number of people were known to have been killed, with the killer still on the loose. After a sleepless night, our family moved further away from the sight of the massacre, into Dunedin.

Like many other families, we would experience the attack as having been directed at the whole community, of which we were a part. People I knew were among the dead. Both professionally and as a neighbour, I played a small role in supporting some of the survivors as well as friends and families of the victims. My closest contact with the massacre came through a patient whom I had been seeing in psychotherapy for a considerable time. One of her few contacts was with her neighbour, Mr A – the man who would later commit the massacre.

After the massacre, my patient suffered great anguish. Not only did she have to cope with having been caught up in the early stages of the massacre together with the deaths of friends and neighbours, but she also feared she was in part responsible, because she had failed to help the killer (whom she had recognised as being in distress). In helping her manage these sources of anxiety, we inevitably revisited what she had known and what she had said to me at various times about the man.

Mr A had always been a rather shy man, not to say withdrawn. When my patient first encountered him a few years earlier, she thought he had shared her generally progressive, anti-authoritarian worldview. When she moved to Aramoana and became reacquainted with him, she realised that whatever his views might once have been, he was now caught up in the cult of survivalism, accompanied – as it so often is – by right-wing extremism. His prior interest in hunting and shooting had developed into a fascination with all things military. His mood was marked by elements of despair and anger, which were sometimes manifested in statements about the pointlessness of life and the maliciousness of so many people. I now know that this information would have rung alarm bells; but I didn't know this then, and nor did anyone else. What my patient saw above all was a sad man who had lost his way and needed help.

At that time, I knew no more about lone-actor massacres than any reasonably well-read person. I was a professor of general psychiatry whose research centred on the long-term impact of child sexual abuse and the causes of domestic violence. Forensic psychiatry was a part-time interest that was soon to become my main area of specialisation. I would take my curiosity about the lone mass killer with me when I moved to Melbourne as Professor of Forensic Psychiatry at Monash University.

From a Texas university campus in 1966 to a primary school in Dunblane, Scotland, in 1996; from Port Arthur in Tasmania in 1996 to Utøya island in Norway in 2011; from the Las Vegas Strip in 2017 and Marjory Stoneman Douglas High School in Parkland, Florida in 2018 to Lewiston, Maine, in 2023 and Örebro, Sweden, in 2025; from vehicular attacks on the streets of Melbourne in 2017 and Toronto in 2018 to Magdeburg, Germany, in 2024: the toll of death and destruction has continued to escalate. The killers all achieved the fame they'd sought, with many of their names still resonating down the years.

Guns have been the usual killing instruments of choice, and by far the deadliest, but knives, bludgeons and motor vehicles are becoming increasingly common. In 1966, I was assessing the Port Arthur killer two days after the massacre when he looked me in the eye and shyly noted that he held the "record" now. He had murdered thirty-five men, women and children. His "record" has long since been surpassed by tragedies such as the 2016 Nice truck massacre (eighty-seven dead and 434 wounded), the 2017 Las Vegas massacre (sixty dead and over 400 wounded) and the 2019 Christchurch massacre (fifty-one killed and forty wounded). It is not just the lethality of these events that is increasing in the Western world, but also the frequency with which they take place. Massacres have occurred throughout human history in the context of military or civil conflict, in which a killer's viciousness is hidden within the anonymity of the group. This book is about a different kind of massacre, in which an armed individual goes out with the intention of killing people, largely chosen at random, usually continuing their attacks until they are themselves killed or captured. The killer's intention is the central feature: the majority of the victims are chosen not because of who they are, but by *where* they are at the time. How many dead and injured are required for such an event to count as a massacre has been much debated, and is relevant to statistical analysis. In this book a general definition will be used, of a number of people injured of whom some are killed. Various terms have been suggested for this type of mass killer. *Lone wolf* is the most unfortunate, with its evocation of a sinister predator to be feared by the common herd: it plays into the fantasies of those who might just act in this manner. *Spree killer* is too jolly for such terrible events. *Autogenic* is too clever by half, and incomprehensible to most readers. *Amok* is a venerable term but perhaps too connected to notions of the exotic Far East. Plain *lone actor* is best.

Lone-actor mass killers are too often confused and conflated with *terrorists*. Some lone-actor killers do gravitate to established extremist groups, giving the appearance of being like-minded; in fact, they float around the periphery, not fitting in, being perceived by the group as 'different' or 'odd'. On the surface, they may appear to be part of a group, but lone actors' true agendas reflect their own highly personalised rage and despair directed at the world in general. They do not kill and die primarily for a collective cause or shared purpose, though they might claim a political or religious motivation. They kill en route to their own destruction as a final rejection of the values of the society of which they were, however unwillingly, a part.

The accounts that follow of killers with whom I have had direct contact use only factual material, available in the public domain, to which I have added my personal responses and interpretations. Some non-essential details in these accounts have been changed in the less notorious cases, to hinder identification. The other cases I discuss are well known, and the names of the perpetrators common knowledge. It may appear silly or an excess of something like political correctness *not* to use their names in this book. But these men, for the most part, killed precisely in the hope of becoming famous. I thus refuse to support their ambitions. More importantly, I hope that news media, in the future, begin refusing to name mass murderers as well, making clear to someone contemplating such acts that they will fail at least in one of their prime motivations – to become infamous. I shall, instead, name some of the victims: the killers discussed in this book murdered hundreds, in total. The names of a handful of these casualties shall have to stand for all those killed and injured.

CHAPTER 1

Face-to-face with a mass killer

ON A WEBSITE that, insightfully, called itself www.conspiracy.com, there was a post on the 'Mysterious Mullen from Monash'. The central claim was that I was party to fabricating the story of the mass shooting in Port Arthur in 1996. The website accused me of being part of a plot to deprive Australians of the right to own guns. The blog suggested some sinister connection between a number of gun massacres and me, in particular at Aramoana in South Island, New Zealand; at Hoddle Street in Melbourne; and at Monash University in the same city. The blogger wrote: "Mullen just happens to have been residing in areas where all the gun massacres have occurred since the late 1980s" and suggested it was unlikely that this was mere coincidence, but was instead part of a plot to fabricate evidence supporting the confiscation of people's guns by governments.

The blog did contain an element of truth. As I have described in the Introduction, I was living just a few miles from Aramoana when a lone perpetrator shot sixteen people, killing thirteen, among whom were people I knew and with whom I had worked. It is also true that I was on the staff at Monash University when the campus shooting there occurred; in fact, the killings took place in a seminar room that, in previous years, had been used regularly for teaching by my wife, Elizabeth. It is also true that I have had long-term contact with the man who committed the 1987 Hoddle Street massacre, in which seven people were killed and nineteen injured – and, as chance would have it, on the same street there is a clinic only a couple of hundred metres away at which I have worked, and which now bears my name. The blogger could have added other coincidences of a similar nature.

There are few other psychiatrists who have had as many opportunities as I have to assess so many lone mass killers. This state of affairs is the product not of some sinister conspiracy, but of where I worked as a forensic psychiatrist. Australia and New Zealand had a spate of mass shootings throughout the 1980s and 1990s. One of the features of these massacres is that, unlike those in other parts of the world, most of the perpetrators survived. They survived not because they surrendered or attempted to escape, but often because courageous people ran at them and disarmed them. In the US, up to 70 per cent of the perpetrators of mass killings have been shot and killed by police, or have had the time to turn their guns on themselves. In the UK, such events have almost always ended in the perpetrators' suicide. In Australasia, most survived the event itself, and thanks to the vigilance of prison officers, they also survived the suicide attempts that almost always occurred in the weeks that followed.

In 1996, like most people in Australia at the time, I first learned of the events at Port Arthur when reports began to appear on the television channels of a mass killing in Tasmania in which thirty-five people had perished. The events of that day shocked the whole Australian community to the core. Just as, a few weeks earlier, the people of Scotland had experienced the Dunblane massacre as a blow to their whole society, virtually every Australian felt personally attacked and hurt. On the morning after the massacre I remember sitting in the sauna at the gym with the usual group of ageing men. The habitual exchange of the trivial and the scandalous was replaced by total silence until one of our number, a onetime sporting hero remembered for rugged indestructibility, tried to speak but ended up in tears – of grief, anger and affront, emotions shared that day with most of our fellow citizens.

A day later, I was contacted by the solicitors for the defence acting for the man charged with these killings, and I travelled to Tasmania to begin my psychiatric examination of him.

When I first examined the killer, in a hospital in Hobart to which he had been moved, he was recovering from the burns he sustained in the final act of the massacre, when he set afire the house in which he was holed up. His intention had been to die in the flames, but when his clothes began to burn he panicked and fled from the house. The police did not shoot him, thinking it was one of the hostages they believed were being held inside. Instead, they saved his life by beating out the flames that were beginning to engulf him.

When I arrived, the Australian media were already gathered at the front of the hospital. Over the next twenty-four hours the numbers of film crews and journalists swelled as news teams flew in from around the world. The killer was on one of the hospital wings that had been cleared of other patients and staff not directly involved in his care. A heavy police presence was established, with all potential entrances to the area guarded. The killer himself was in a small side ward, with armed police both inside and outside the room. The police made no objection to withdrawing from the room at my request, though they did make a point of ensuring that I had a buzzer at hand that, in normal times, was used to summon nursing staff. They emphasised that they would be listening, and at the first buzz would be there to rescue me along with the social worker who was present in the early part of the interview. Objectively, the man presented no threat, but the police assumed that I would appreciate the reassurance.

People who know I spend time alone with homicide offenders ask whether or not I am afraid of being attacked. By the time I see such offenders they are all powerless, however, and most are frightened by what is happening to them – and what might happen. They see me as a doctor who may or may not be of help, but who is unlikely to harm them, whereas what I see is not a *killer* but a *person who has killed*, and who is usually now vulnerable. I am not confronted by the person they were when wielding the knife, pointing the gun or clutching for their victim's throat. It is far more difficult to look beyond the horror of the offence to see the perpetrators in their social contexts; understanding the *who* and *why* becomes impossible when we are so dazzled by the horror of their actions that the human being responsible for them becomes invisible.

Occasionally, in these encounters, I have been threatened, but I have never been attacked. (When I have been physically attacked in my professional life, I was most often working as a young doctor in an emergency room, or trying to examine brain-damaged, delirious patients on general hospital wards.) There are exceptions: some do try to be intimidating, and it is unwise to provoke them unnecessarily or strike a confrontational pose. But that is true if you want to avoid trouble in many human interactions, particularly if you are, as I am, a large male with a broken nose and far from gentle appearance.

I always prefer – in fact, insist on – interviewing perpetrators in private. On this occasion, the social worker present for the initial period was someone the Port Arthur killer knew well, and trusted. I hoped her presence would provide some reassurance for him. He was partially restrained by leather straps attaching him to the bed. This made me uncomfortable; it must have made him even *more* uncomfortable. There was considerable reluctance from the police to remove the straps, despite my requests. The only two times I have previously been forced to evaluate someone while they were in restraints concerned a man in the Guantánamo Bay detention camp and a man suspected of being an IRA terrorist, who had been injured during arrest and was subsequently strapped to a hospital bed. (It turned out he was not a terrorist, but a CIA operative.) At least in Hobart there was some excuse, given the nature and recent occurrence of the killings. In Guantánamo, manacling the man and chaining him to the floor was simply a matter of following regulations: he presented no conceivable danger of attacking me or his lawyer, whom he admired and trusted.

"I've got the record, haven't I?" was almost the first question the Port Arthur killer asked. I did not need to ask which record he was referring to. On 28 April 1996 he had shot fifty-five people, of whom thirty-five were fatally wounded and many others left with terrible injuries. Among the dead were Joanne Winter and her fifteen-month-old son; Kate Scott, twenty-two; and Madeline Mykac, three. It was the worst single episode of mass murder by a lone gunman, and this dreadful 'record' stood until 2011, when the massacre on the Norwegian island of Utøya saw sixty-nine people killed.

Most of the Port Arthur victims were holidaymakers. The site contains the ruins of a large prison colony dating back to the nineteenth century, and despite its grim associations, it is one of Australia's most popular tourist destinations. The victims of the shooting came from all around Australia, and a few were overseas visitors. Many were there in family groups, and among those killed were a number of children, including two sisters aged three and six.

Details of the massacre as told by those who survived evoke images of pure horror. The survivors described the killer laughing and smiling in delight as he went about destroying the lives of people helpless to protect themselves and their families. This image is the most enduring one for me. At one point, he pushed aside an injured mother to kill her child, whom she was trying to protect with her own body. He stalked a small child running away in fear to shoot her down, reportedly laughing throughout.

The Australian media struggled to give expression to both distress and the need to understand what had happened. They inevitably turned to the words *evil*, *unholy*, *monster* and *insane*, used singly or in combination. The conservative newspaper *The Australian* ran a front-page picture of the murderer doctored to transmute the bland features of the actual man into a suitably eye-piercing image of a devil. It is easy to criticise these responses with the benefit of distance and hindsight, but at the time they were part of a genuine cry of collective distress and anger.

The killer survived to deny, rationalise, and occasionally attempt to glorify his murderous behaviour. He had difficulty telling his story. Being incapable of creating a coherent account, he produced only disconnected revelations and occasional inadvertent insights, which were infused with contradictions and riddled with self-serving fabrications. In the videos of the police interrogations, which have now been made public, he is seen laughing and giggling while at one moment he denies involvement, and in the next points to himself as the culprit. He is shown repeatedly asking the police to tell him how many were killed, with an expression it is difficult not to see as gleeful. Although he is a living witness his story has to be constructed as much from the accounts of others as from anything he has said or ever will be able to say.

He was born in 1966, the eldest child of a couple who emigrated from England to Tasmania. Apart from being somewhat slow in developing motor movements and speech, his early childhood was unremarkable. However, when he started to attend nursery and preschool, concerns were raised. In the company of other children he seemed incapable of entering into shared activities or participating effectively in games. He was described by teachers and childcare workers as aggressive, restless and destructive. Almost as soon as he started at primary school at age five, he was referred for assessment by an educational psychologist. This was to be the first of many such evaluations over the next decade.

The assessments and suggested remedial measures shifted over the years, but the problems remained the same or became worse. Ignoring attempts to control him and responding to discipline with defiance, the restless boy appeared fearless and, as a result, was in constant danger of hurting himself. He was disliked and avoided by other children, whom he tormented if given a chance. There were repeated accounts of him torturing animals, and fears were expressed about his destructiveness and, in particular, about the way he treated his younger sister. As the years went by, stealing, lying and even occasional arson were added to the roster.

A relatively consistent story is told by the records from schools, child guidance clinics, educational psychologists and even fellow pupils recalling the killer as a schoolboy. Not surprisingly, he had a totally different perspective. He recalled his school days with loathing, believing himself stigmatised, rejected, humiliated and bullied by his peers and harassed by teachers, always being blamed for whatever went wrong. He claimed he was "hazed", knocked around all the time, and that no one wanted to be his friend. He experienced his teachers as ganging up against him. He said he fabricated symptoms of illness out of terror at having to return to school. He remembered himself as the victim of other children, just as the teachers recall him as the tormentor and troublemaker.

The professionals attempting to counsel, treat or otherwise guide the youngster suggested various explanations for his disturbed behaviour. His parents, particularly his mother, attracted a considerable number of negative comments. But their only other child was developing normally, despite having to cope with her elder brother, and would grow up a perfectly functional woman.

What emerges from the contemporary account, aside from theoretically driven judgements and attributions of blame, is the story of a couple struggling to cope with a very difficult child. He was diagnosed with the forerunner of attention deficit hyperactivity disorder (ADHD) and placed on medication. This reportedly improved things for a time, but appears not to have been continued. Special diets were tried – without effect, except in the eyes of their proponents. Counsellors and family therapists came and went, but he continued on his lonely path of disruption.

Over the years a series of intelligence tests were carried out, the results of which consistently indicated that he was mildly intellectually impaired. Testing performed after the massacre suggest he fell into the lowest 2 per cent of the population across the range of intellectual functions. His parents, particularly his father, had experienced great difficulty accepting this, and had resisted attempts to shift his son into any form of special schooling. To be fair to the father, his son appeared to be an attractive, lively boy. Throughout his childhood and early adult life, the future killer had the kind of good looks that suggest to the casual observer normal, if not superior, abilities. The dramatic contrast between what his looks appeared to promise and what he could deliver bedevilled him throughout his life.

A brief film taken by a local television station of the boy at the age of twelve survives. He was interviewed about having suffered burns when he had 'accidentally' set off a collection of fireworks. It is impossible to avoid contaminating the image of this little boy with the knowledge of what is to come. Even so, he presents a curious picture of self-possession and suppressed glee as he recounts what sounds suspiciously like a pack of lies. Could this have been a moment when, for this eventual murderer, links began to form between fame and acts of destruction?

He was transferred from school to school after exclusions, but – in no small part owing to the efforts of his father – he finally left school with basic literacy. It soon became clear, however, that he would never be able to fulfil the demands of open employment. In 1984 he was assessed for eligibility for a disability pension by an experienced psychiatrist, Dr Eric Cunningham-Dax, who concluded that he was personality-disordered and intellectually limited. The psychiatrist also raised the possibility that, given the level of his interpersonal difficulties and the oddities in his manner, he might in the future develop a schizophrenic illness. Another psychiatrist described him as "an inconsequential young man with short attention span and a grasshopper mind".

For reasons that are not clear from the records, his general practitioner came to the conclusion that he had paranoid schizophrenia. This doctor even prescribed antipsychotic medication for a short period. In fact, there was no real basis for a diagnosis of schizophrenia, and neither of the psychiatrists who had assessed him found evidence for such a psychosis. This tentative suggestion about a future possibility was later understandably interpreted by the mother as a firm diagnosis of schizophrenia in her son. When, after the massacre, this 'diagnosis' was made public, it fostered a period of misinformed public debate and understandable distress for those with this illness and their support and advocacy groups.

The Port Arthur killer might well have remained a strange, solitary man eking out a life on the margins of society except for what can only be described as an extraordinary series of events. His father managed to organise gardening and odd jobs for his son around the neighbourhood, which provided a semblance of useful employment. In 1986, he met one Helen Mary Elizabeth Harvey, who made use of his gardening services. Harvey was an eccentric heiress to part of a fortune left by Australia's most successful bookie. She lived with her elderly mother and, until this man came into her life, she led a solitary existence, but for over forty cats, fourteen dogs and some fifty caged birds. The cats and dogs, reportedly, ran wild through her property in an environment of chaotic squalor.

The relationship between Harvey and the future killer attracted considerable speculation after the massacre; much of it was as fanciful as it was scurrilous. His account, and those of a few people who might actually know, suggest that he evoked the maternal feelings in Harvey that had previously been lavished on cats, dogs and various other assorted creatures. He, in some ways, was an ideal child substitute – an attractive, blonde, blue-eyed overgrown cherub. He retained the restless enthusiasm of a child, and – perhaps most importantly – the insatiable appetite for a mutuality of fawning attention, of which only dogs and some small children are capable. His role was to revel in a round of outings, treats and parties organised for him by Harvey. He obtained a second chance at childhood, with a new 'mother', with no school or other children to mar the days, no expectations other than enjoyment ... and certainly no discipline. There seem to have been very few limits, if any, on the flow of indulgences, which ranged from parties to overseas holidays. He later described Harvey to me as having been the only real friend he had ever had, as someone who shared his interests and, perhaps surprisingly, as someone whom he could help.

Harvey and her mother did require considerable help, as they seemed incapable of managing even basic self-care: one from age and infirmity, the other from peculiarities of personality if not frank mental illness. The younger Harvey may well have had a chronic schizophrenic disorder, and she seems to have received intermittent psychiatric care in previous years. The future killer's father brought a degree of organisation to the chaos of the home, and his mother became drawn into the Harvey household as a cleaner and carer for Harvey's mother. Following the death of the elderly woman, a small farm was purchased near Hobart and the range of animals expanded to include horses, donkeys, sheep, some cows and a pig (the latter reportedly taking up residence in the house).

This bucolic idyll ended abruptly in 1993 when the car Harvey was driving, with the future Port Arthur gunman and a number of dogs as passengers, crashed. Harvey was killed, and the man seriously injured. He recovered from his injuries to learn that he had inherited Harvey's two properties and the income from a substantial trust fund. Overnight, the twenty-six-year-old was a property-owning millionaire.

He was barely numerate, and his capacity to manage money was limited. He went on the type of spending spree you might expect from a young man of previously limited resources suddenly presented with what must have seemed inexhaustible wealth, and it included clothes, electronic gizmos, games, holidays and expensive meals. To this was added the acquisition of guns ... and then more guns. On one occasion he paid over AUD 5,000 for a pump-action shotgun that he particularly desired.

The father made great efforts advising his son to structure his finances and ensure some secure, ongoing income stream. To this end, the young man's newfound wealth was placed in the hands of a government organisation that manages the estates for those incapable of handling their own affairs. The father's efforts ended upon his death from suicide, or perhaps the suicide followed the completion of the arrangements for his son.

The father's death was re-examined following the massacre, as was the death of Harvey and any number of unsolved murders in Tasmania over the previous years. The fact that no plausible evidence emerged for the Port Arthur killer's involvement in any of these deaths did not stop rumours and media 'revelations' that he had killed his father, his benefactor and other victims. It was as if there was a need to find a trail of murderous violence that culminated in the terrible massacre – a trail that would somehow make more understandable both the ultimate tragedy, and the man himself. The father's suicide was, in fact, remarkable only for the care he took both in putting his affairs in order, leaving apologetic letters and planning his death by drowning. Why he killed himself is uncertain and was not clarified by the suicide notes. Whatever the reason, with his father's death, the son lost the source of the structure that had been built around him to both protect him from the world he couldn't cope with, and to control his more irresponsible behaviours.

Wealth may not automatically bring happiness, but it does usually bring a wider range of options – and that, at least, affords the opportunity for a fuller life. How, then, did this young man's metamorphosis from welfare recipient to gentleman of independent means end up in tragedy for so many people? Some parts of the puzzle are obvious. Having a large disposable income removed any financial restraints on his passion for guns, and facilitated a new vice: drinking regularly and to excess. It also expanded opportunities to overcome his interpersonal failures and humiliating rejections. Money bought him some friends and occasional sexual partners, but even he had the sense sooner or later to recognise that he was being exploited. He may well have become more, rather than less, sensitive to people pretending to be friendly for what they could get. This perceptiveness would have been accentuated, given his idealised notions about friendship and intense desire to recreate the kind of intimacy he'd experienced with Harvey. In any case, the hangers-on likely didn't stay around long after discovering that his wealth was all tied up in trusts that provided a monthly income, but no access to capital. The young man's lack of money-management skills resulted, on a monthly basis, in extravagant spending leading to his going broke, creating a cycle of humiliation and imposed discipline that he found infuriating. Moreover, having all the appurtenances of a good life made his continual social failures all the more galling.

He was wealthy, but lived alone in a large house. His mother visited and tried to advise and guide him, but seems to have remained largely impotent in influencing her son during the three years that remained between the deaths of Harvey and his father and the massacre at Port Arthur. In those years, he became a familiar figure around Hobart's restaurants, cafés, clothing shops, video shops and, above all, travel agencies. He acquired a Volvo and a surfboard, which became a permanent fixture on the roof of the car. It was more a style statement than actual gear; he looked the part, with flowing blonde hair and a tan, but in fact, he lacked the persistence needed to acquire any but the most basic surfing skills.

Those three years were punctuated by ten overseas trips, the last of which was to the UK in January 1996. These excursions nearly all ended in his returning earlier than originally planned. Several lasted only a matter of days, with the bulk of the time taken up sitting in airplanes. He explained to me that his peregrinations were, for him, a chance to "meet up with normal people", but "it didn't work". He travelled to places such as London, Los Angeles, Amsterdam and Bangkok, where he would go to what he described as "cafeterias" and try to start conversations with people eating there. He received, hardly surprisingly, repeated rebuffs, varying from polite requests to go away to angry rejections and complaints. (The most frequent response entailed the person being approached – usually a young woman on her own –getting up and either leaving or moving to another table.)

Though he had difficulties recalling his impressions of the various cities he'd visited, he could list in some detail his repeated abortive attempts to engage people in conversation. Each episode was angrily recounted as evidence of the malevolent refusal of people to accept him. He claimed that there had only been two really good aspects to his globetrotting: the sex shops of central Amsterdam and the conversations he was able to have with various people seated next to him on international flights. The police managed to trace a number of his seatmates on these flights. All remembered him; most recalled a gauche, intrusive young man who tried repeatedly to engage them in conversation using a mixture of inappropriate personal questions or equally dubious self-disclosures. Two women reported that he had not only attempted to arrange to meet them after they landed, but had proposed marriage. For him, these were treasured memories of shared friendship. The imposed proximity equated, in his mind, with the uncritical attention that Harvey had once provided. It is, however, unlikely that those belted up next to him through many hours of flying have similarly fond memories of the attention they received. Can there be any more pathetic image of failed interpersonal intimacy than the cherishing of memories of the enforced closeness to strangers created by international air travel?

He gave a variety of accounts about when, and for what reason, he began planning to commit a massacre. He acknowledged that for years he had entertained violent fantasies consisting of a mixture of heroic last stands and revenge scenarios. When the police searched his house after the killings, a collection of VHS tapes were found. These fell into two broad groups, children's movies such as *The Lion King*, which he nominated as his all-time favourite, and violent, lone-hero films such as *Rambo*. (He had named his pet parrot "Rambo".) There were multiple copies of some of these films, presumably either purchased in error or out of an enthusiasm to repeat the pleasures of acquiring the desired object.

He dated his fascination with guns back to going shooting with his father when he was a boy, though there are reasons to suspect this may have been more wishful thinking than accurate recall. (His mother stated that her late husband had an abhorrence of guns, and would never have had them in the house.) Nevertheless, as a boy he had earned pocket money from shooting and selling rabbits around the neighbourhood, suggesting there was at least one .22 around the parents' property.

He began buying guns after coming into his inheritance from Harvey. He'd never had a gun licence – but this fact, in his account, appears only to have upped the price asked by gun dealers rather than diminishing their willingness to supply him. He acquired a small arsenal of sporting and military weaponry, including some semi- and fully automatic guns. He demonstrated a reasonably extensive knowledge of the guns he had owned, and of guns in general, and explained at length why he had chosen the weapons he'd taken with him to Port Arthur. These had not included the fully automatic machine gun he owned, which he considered too unreliable because of its tendency to jam. In the year or so prior to the killings, he had regularly gone shooting in the extensive forests and wilderness which surround his hometown, Hobart. He admitted that he had fantasised about killing people when discharging the weapons at trees and rocks, and made extravagant claims for his abilities as a marksman.

Like so many of the men who progress to committing a mass shooting he was well aware of some of the precedents. Despite having only a basic education and a paucity of general knowledge, he spoke in detail about a number of previous massacres, such as those at Hoddle Street in Melbourne and the 1966 University of Texas shooting. His claim to have the "record" spoke to the level of his knowledge about the killers he had sought to emulate. However, it was as much from films that he created his model of slaughter.

As with a number of other mass shooters, he prefaced the massacre by killing specific victims: a couple called David and Noelene Martin. He claimed that they had greatly harmed his father and thus his whole family by buying a piece of land near Port Arthur. The family mythology seems to have been that his father had been in the process of purchasing this land when his then-friends, the Martins, to whom he had enthused about the property, stepped in and outbid him. He claimed that both he and his father had subsequently tried without success to purchase the land from the Martins. In his view of the world, this event had changed the course of his father's life for the worse, and brought numerous disasters down upon the family. He claimed he had thought repeatedly about killing the Martins long before the notion of committing a massacre had entered his head.

Exactly when he determined to commit the massacre and began planning it never became entirely clear. He denied that reports of the

Dunblane massacre earlier in the year played any role, though the vehemence of his denials raised in me some doubts. He reported that at least six weeks earlier, he had decided on a date for the killings and circled the selected day on his calendar. This simple gesture became significant in overcoming his later doubts, because he felt that he had made a firm commitment by performing it.

One of the twists in the long story was that while he was planning and preparing for the massacre, he met a young woman with whom he appears to have developed not just a sexual relationship but one of mutual affection. His preoccupation with carrying out a murderous spectacle diminished, and after the event he had difficulty explaining why he had not abandoned his preparations. One explanation he offered was that because the date had been marked on the calendar, he was in some way compelled to carry through with his murderous commitment. This smacks of the rigidity and magical thinking of the obsessive.

The term *obsessional* would not spring to mind as a prominent characteristic of this untidy, often disorganised man. There were, however, marked rigidities in his behaviour, and a preoccupation with details as well as a predisposition to repetitive rumination. I may be overemphasising these traits because obsessional features have been so prominent in some of the other lone-actor mass killers I have examined. It seems to me that obsessiveness plays a part in enabling many of these killers both to plan in such detail and to carry through with those plans, indifferent to the pain and terror of their victims. (The philosopher Mary Midgley suggests that obsession carries with it a tendency for a person's other interests and commitments, not involved in whatever serves as their obsessive preoccupation, to atrophy and die. She considers that to allow an obsession to take over is to consent to some degree both to one's own death and to the death of others.)

I was never able to pin down exactly when he moved from a general intention to wreak revenge on those he believed had harmed and humiliated him to a firm commitment to kill. One thing was clear: he said it followed a decision to kill himself. The suicidal idea probably peaked after the breakdown of one of his less ephemeral sexual relationships. There were also escalating frustrations created by his repeated social failures and his increasing inability to exert control over his money. The plan he developed was for murder-suicide. He expected to die in a dramatic gun battle with police at Port Arthur. He confidently expected his actions to make him world-famous, which, indeed, they did.

The Port Arthur killer had considerable difficulty responding to enquiries into his psychological and emotional states, reflecting not an unwillingness to disclose his internal world of thoughts and feelings, but simply the limited vocabulary at his disposal. His silly sense of humour was also a bar to exploring the presence of a serious form of psychopathology. For example, when asked if he had ever experienced the radio and television talking directly to him or about him, he told me with great delight that he was now famous, so of course *everyone* was talking about him. Similarly, attempts to explore the possibility of grandiose or religious delusions were productive mainly of the childish jokes he enjoyed making.

The one area of abnormality in his mental state that did emerge was a marked tendency to oversensitivity and self-reference. He was suspicious of nearly everyone as being not only aligned against him, but taking pleasure in inflicting harassment and humiliation upon him. In public places, he had long felt that people talked about him and laughed at him behind his back. He even sometimes believed that he heard the insults and imprecations that they were uttering. He believed that most people avoided him and rejected his attempts at being friendly with the specific intention of causing him distress. He could not explain *why* he was the victim of such frequent unpleasantness, other than it was just how people usually were. He did not think he was the victim of organised persecution. Alongside his sense of being a victim, there was also a strong sense of being *special*. He believed himself to be not just as good as other people but to be their superior in almost all areas. Part of the antagonism with which he felt surrounded, he was convinced, came from envy of his abilities, his good looks and, latterly, his wealth. In his mind, at least, he was handsome, wealthy and, if not wise, at least as clever as the next person.

He spoke almost casually about having decided to kill himself some weeks prior to the massacre. These suicidal intentions did not seem to have emerged in the context of any major change in his mood, but rather on the basis of a long-standing sense of frustration and general unhappiness. He had felt trapped in a cycle of victimisation from which he could not escape. Life, he felt, had become intolerable despite his financial and other advantages. He gave no history of the types of changes found in severe depression. There were no marked alterations to his sleep pattern, appetite or ability to concentrate. The only change he reported had been the increasing anger and determination to seek revenge while proving to the world he was someone important.

Diagnostically he did not have a schizophrenic illness, nor any other form of psychotic disorder. He did not have major depression. The suggestion that he might have what was then more widely called Asperger's syndrome, was suggested by one of the psychiatrists who assessed him. The killer was certainly socially incompetent and lacking much appreciation for the feelings of others, but his developmental history, which had been well documented, was not marked by any of the abnormalities specific to the autism spectrum disorders of which that syndrome is one. He was not unconcerned about others and their view of him; on the contrary, he was constantly anxious about the actions and supposed feelings of others towards him. We know he was intellectually impaired, being in the mild to moderate range of disability, and intensely resentful about the way he had been treated by the world. We know that he had, for many years, entertained violent fantasies of vengeance and heroic last stands.

What was he seeking on that April morning, when he loaded the guns into his Volvo and drove off towards Port Arthur? He wanted to be killed. He wanted his death to conform to the fantasy he had of the lone gunman fighting and dying gloriously. He wanted revenge on a persecuting and rejecting world. Above all, he wanted celebrity and personal vindication.

It is difficult to believe so many were killed and injured because a rigid, dim young man lacked the ability to change his plans. Experience has taught me that it takes trivial as well as profound influences to come together in the tragedy of murder, each element playing a greater or lesser role, but each in its own way causal. The only comfort is that if murder – any kind of murder – is the result of multiple factors, then there is a multiplicity of opportunities to stop the fatal progress. This is, of course, far truer of planned killings than of the majority of murders, which occur as impulsive acts by impassioned, frightened and intoxicated perpetrators. But even there, the fatal act is a product of a concatenation of influences, any of which could have been changed so as to prevent the progress to murder.

The man's barrister, John Avery, performed a notable service for the Australian community in the days leading up to the trial by dissuading his client from pleading *not guilty*: no easy task, given that the killer was still angry, still bent on maximising his shot at fame. As the trial approached, the man had begun to speak enthusiastically of the prospect of becoming the centre of world media attention. This played into his fantasies of glory as the powerful, avenging hero. Had he pleaded *not guilty*, that would not only have provided a platform for him to express his resentment, but would have precipitated a lengthy trial in which many of the survivors of the massacre would have been dragged through the horror of bearing witness in front of the court and the world media.

The brief, low-key trial that resulted from the *guilty* plea contrasts with the circus that occurred in Oslo fifteen years later with the trial of the Utøya killer. Had the Port Arthur killer persisted in instructing his barrister to plead *not guilty*, then the only way to prevent a full-scale trial would have been to have him declared unfit to be tried. The instructions the man was giving his barrister were to plead *guilty* to some of the charges and *not guilty* to others: there was neither a rational nor a legal basis for the distinction he wished to make between the killings he admitted and those he denied. His claims were childish, based on assertions that kept fluctuating in nature, linked only by their silliness. One of the criteria for "fitness" is the capacity of the accused to provide meaningful instructions to his or her lawyers. Another is that this inability derives from some mental disorder or mental incapacity.

In the Port Arthur killer, either his intellectual deficiency or his psychiatric state would have had to be presented to the court in a manner that satisfied the legal criteria for incapacity, though it would have involved stretching a point. Fortunately, this situation did not arise. (In my opinion, had he persisted in wanting to plead *not guilty*, declaring him unfit would have been a proper course to follow for the sake of the victims and the wider community.) Later, I shall discuss the importance of not allowing such killers the opportunity to strut and self-glorify in the glare of publicity.

The Port Arthur killer has spent nearly thirty years in prison. He was isolated from other prisoners for much of that time, for his own safety. He has spent considerable periods in the prison's psychiatric unit. This is also where he would have finished up if found unfit to plead. The punishment of imprisonment is intended to be the deprivation of liberty – just that. Occasionally, more viciously inclined prison officers sometimes seem to fail to understand this principle. In this killer's case, at least in the early days of his incarceration, various humiliations and intimidation were inflicted on the now-helpless man. These practices, I am assured, have long since ceased. He is now an obese, irate man who looks much older than his years. He had too few personal resources to live well when free and wealthy. In prison, he has little or no ability to lighten the burden of lifelong detention. To date, his attempts at suicide have failed. The future for him is more of the same – or, to be precise, a continuing *nothing* of an existence.

I have no sympathy for the man responsible for the killing and maiming of so many people, and have no doubt that he should remain in prison for the rest of his life. However, when I have visited him in prison over the years, I cannot avoid some feelings of sadness at seeing someone reduced to such a shambling wreck of a human being.

The community's shock and outrage in response to the Port Arthur massacre was translated by the Australian government into legislation to control the type of military-style weapons the killer had used. A gun buyback also aimed to remove military-style weapons from circulation. The effects of these initiatives have now been thoroughly evaluated. Mass shootings, which, up to that time, had occurred more frequently in Australia than in the US on a population basis, virtually ceased after 1997. Furthermore, all gun deaths from homicide have dramatically decreased. The massacre at Port Arthur brought about an end to tolerance for people wishing to own weapons the purpose of which lay outside sport and hunting. Australia is a safer place today as a result.

CHAPTER 2

Running amok

OVER THE PAST century, the Western world has experienced the gradual emergence of the lone mass killer. This form of murderous violence was new to our culture. It is characterised by a lone killer (or, on rare occasions, a couple working together), entering a public space in a carefully planned action and slaughtering people at random. In Western nations, the weapon of choice has almost always been the gun. The killer usually continues with his (for it is almost always a *he*) murderous rampage until he is either gunned down or turns his weapon on himself, terminating both his life and the carnage. So horribly familiar has this scenario become that it is difficult to grasp that such behaviour has not always been a part of our social landscape.

This behaviour may be new to the West, but something similar has been seen in other cultures at other times. The sixteenth-century adventurer Duarte Barbosa described, in an account of his travels in the Far East, a strange phenomenon called *amok* (or *amuk*) among the Javanese inhabitants of the Malay Peninsula. He wrote that episodes of *amok* involved a young man running out into public spaces armed with a spear or an axe, and killing – apparently at random – anyone he encountered. This usually continued until the killer was overpowered, and almost always killed.

Amok was considered by subsequent Western writers as a curious, totally foreign piece of Eastern exotica. Descriptions make clear that the objective of the perpetrator, called the *pengamuk*, was to force people to kill him.

There were two parts to an episode of *amok*. The first involved the *pengamuk* attacking and attempting to kill people in a public place, often a market. The second required other men gathering together to beat and stab the *pengamuk* to death. The first part was a public assertion of the killer's power; the second was the attainment of a death that was not suicide. The frequency of these events attested to the attraction for despondent, despairing young men who felt rejected and humiliated by those around them of a form of suicide that was not an act of withdrawal and defeat, but one of heroic personal assertion and vengeance. In becoming a *pengamuk*, such people avoided the strong religious prohibition against self-murder by provoking others to kill them.

The British colonial administration, towards the end of the nineteenth century, attempted to reduce the frequency of men running *amok* by disrupting this well-established cultural script. They did this by denying a *pengamuk* his final objective of finishing up dead. Preventing the *pengamuk* killing anyone was difficult; capturing him alive was simpler. The police were issued with tools designed to assist in this aim. One was a long-handled instrument resembling a two-pronged pitchfork with the spikes placed wide enough apart to go round the offender's neck. This was used to pin the *pengamuk* against some convenient wall. Another was a somewhat more elaborate contraption consisting of a steel hoop at the end of a long pole. The hoop was intended to be brought down around the body of the *pengamuk* and tightened using an attachment to the pole. The point of this policy was to deprive the *pengamuk* of the satisfaction of having someone kill him.

The other change in policy was to encourage courts to opt for committing these men to a psychiatric hospital on the grounds of insanity, rather than hanging them as murderers. The old colonial lunatic asylum at Johor Bahru (now in Malaysia), which still functions, has a building originally constructed to house those *pengamuk* found insane. This unit is now a secure ward for the detention of mentally abnormal offenders committed by the courts. In the Malay culture at that time, to be labelled as mad and committed to an asylum was a matter of great shame both for individuals and for their families. In a stroke, 'shameful incarceration' was substituted for a supposedly 'honourable death'. The policy was credited as bringing about the virtual disappearance of *amok* in Malaya.

Some years prior to the introduction of the 'capture-not-kill approach', in 1846, Sir William Norris, Chief Justice of Ceylon (now Sri Lanka), was in little doubt about sentencing to death a man named Sunam, who had run amok, killing eight people: "The atrocities are of a peculiar character, such as are never perpetuated by Christians, Hindus, Chinese, or any other class than Mohammedans, especially Malays, among whom it is frightfully common." These "fiendish exercises" the Chief Justice considered, arose from "fanaticism, superstition, overweening pride, or from all combined."

In 1893, Dr William Gilmore Ellis, the superintendent of one of the Malay lunatic asylums, gave an account of the genesis of "the amok of the Malays". He suggested that it began with a peculiar condition of mind: *sakit-hati*, literally "heart sickness". Characterised by brooding over supposed wrongs and the possibility of revenge, this state then progresses to suicidal feelings. Dr Ellis wrote: "Many Malays have told me that they consider amok a kind of suicide ... A man, from some cause or other, considers life not worth living; suicide is a heinous sin in Islam, therefore the amok acts in the hope of his being killed."

Subsequent research has made it clear that '*amok*-like' behaviours were not confined to Malays, but occur in a range of cultural groups in Southeast Asia and parts of sub-Saharan Africa. What seems common to the various types of *amok* is what could be termed a *cultural script*, in which a male who has suffered a loss of prestige or been overwhelmed by a sense of frustration and hopelessness turns for vindication and escape towards this violent form of murder-suicide. Like all forms of complex human behaviour, these massacres usually represent the coming together of a variety of factors, none in itself sufficient to explain the activity, but each in its different way essential to the outcome. A despairing man enraged with the world he blames for his misery emerges as an important part of these tales of mass murder.

It is possible to extract from the writings about *amok* during the colonial period a picture of the factors commonly characterising the *pengamuk*. These include:

- Male gender
- Aged late teens and twenties
- Coming from a reasonably prosperous home background
- Unpartnered, without many friends
- Blaming others and society at large for their failures in life
- Having experienced recent humiliations and setbacks
- Having become even more withdrawn than usual in the weeks and months before the attack
- Having spoken of life not being worth living, and possibly of thoughts of suicide
- Not usually having a history of violence or other offending
- Being part of a culture with a script for suicide and some form of redemption through killing people at random.

These features will turn up again and again in the case histories in this book.

The British colonial administration in the Malaysian Peninsula had success in reducing the incidence of *amuk* by capturing the *pengamuk* alive, thereby preventing him from transforming his act into the semblance of being killed in battle. Today's lone mass killers also seek to transform suicide into a triumphant act of self-assertion. Weakness and withdrawal are transmuted into strength and aggression. Suicide is no longer a quiet, lonely end, but a loud, public spectacle. The killers do not disappear from the world, but grab the attention of that world. They seek to go in a flash of infamy, raging into the dark.

Yet this book will also examine how we act and react with regard to lone mass killers who have *already* embarked on their deadly missions – and highlight how our responses during and after the attacks might dissuade others from taking a similar course.

CHAPTER 3

Amok comes to the West

MASSACRES ARE AS much a part of the Western world's history as that of other cultures –perhaps more so. Two of the earliest examples of the lone-actor massacre in the Western world in modern times were a teacher at a school in Germany and an ex-soldier studying at the University of Texas.

The first case took place in 1913, in the small German town of Mühlhausen, near Stuttgart. What was new was that an individual acted alone, pursuing his own idiosyncratic agenda, killing victims chosen largely at random, in expectation of the drama ending in his own death. Ernst Wagner was not following a pattern he had learned from the behaviour of others. As far as we know, he lacked any knowledge of *amok* or such projects of murder-suicide in other cultures. He wrote an original script for himself. His originality stemmed quite simply from madness. Until recently, Wagner was remembered only within the covers of obscure psychiatric texts as a prime example of paranoia or, as it is now termed, delusional disorder.

On 3 September 1913, Wagner cut the throats of his wife and four children as they lay sleeping. He then armed himself with two Mauser pistols and a supply of ammunition, and travelled by train to the village of Mühlhausen. There, during the night, he started a number of fires in barns and outhouses. As the villagers woke from their sleep and ran to try to put out the flames, he began shooting at men, chosen at random. Wagner shot twenty men, eight of whom died on the spot, before a courageous group of villagers managed to disarm and capture him.

Wagner was a well-educated man with literary ambitions. He had kept a journal and written numerous poems over many years. Immediately before launching his murderous project, Wagner took these writings to a local professor of German literature with whom he had a slight acquaintance, assuring him that they would soon be of great literary and historic significance. Subsequently a psychiatrist, Robert Gaupp, was able to trace in these writings both the emergence of Wagner's paranoid illness and the development of his plan for mass murder and suicide. They had been in development for several years, and the final enactment had been planned down to the minutest detail. Had he fully succeeded, his plan would have culminated in a death worthy of a grand opera. He planned, after the killings at Mühlhausen, to set alight the tower of the nearby castle at Ludwigsburg and to die by self-immolation in the flames of this immense funeral pyre. In the event, his dream ended in capture, trial and – on his being found insane – incarceration in the state asylum of Winnental until his death in 1938.

Wagner was born in 1874 in Eglosheim, a former village that was becoming incorporated as a suburb of the city of Ludwigsburg. He was the ninth of ten children in a farming family. His father, who was reportedly an alcoholic, died when Wagner was still a child. Wagner's mother was described as an irresponsible woman, morally lax, prone to chronic complaining and litigiousness. She had several close relatives who suffered severe mental illnesses. Despite what must have been a troubled home life, Wagner grew up a bright, imaginative child who excelled academically. His abilities obtained him a scholarship to a teacher training college.

Gaupp suggests that Wagner was a self-conscious young man, pedantic, prone to arrogance and given to pessimism. Wagner's autobiographical writings chronicle his increasing preoccupation, from eighteen years of age, with masturbation, both the practice and the supposed ill effects of the indulgence. Though reassured by a doctor whom he consulted, Wagner continued to believe his onanism would damage him physically and psychologically. More sinister was, however, his increasing preoccupation with the notion that others could detect evidence of this secret vice in his appearance – though, to be fair, many an adolescent has experienced such anxieties. In his case, however, self-consciousness progressed to believing that his fellow students repeatedly made oblique references to his masturbation and discussed and laughed about it when he was not with them.

In 1901, Wagner took up a teaching position in Mühlhausen. In his writings he describes an evening sometime after his arrival in this rural town when, after having drunk a considerable quantity of beer at a local inn, he went to a nearby barn and committed bestiality there. (The exact type of farm animal he assaulted is not revealed.) When he awoke the following morning he was mortified by the memory of the previous night. Apparently, his intense guilt continued, increasing rather than decreasing over the subsequent months. He began to worry that he might have been seen, or that his secret could be divined from his appearance and manner. Gradually, he became convinced that the villagers knew of his act of bestiality and were discussing it and mocking him. He purchased a revolver, which he carried with him constantly for the sole purpose of shooting himself should he be denounced, or should the police come to arrest him.

Wagner's state of torment seems to have been relieved, at least temporarily, when he began a relationship with the innkeeper's daughter, whom he later married. They moved from Mühlhausen when he was appointed to a more senior position at a school in a suburb of Stuttgart. His fears of being exposed as a sexual deviant seem to have gone into partial abeyance for a time, but they were later to recur and intensify. In 1904 he became convinced that his sexual indiscretion was again being talked about by those with whom he worked. He believed that villagers from Mühlhausen were deliberately spreading word of his transgression in the barn, and were otherwise acting to destroy his reputation and undermine his position as a teacher. Wagner attributed his failure to find a publisher for his poems, plays and novels to the same cause.

When Wagner's beliefs about this persecution became public after his arrest, extensive enquiries were made among the surviving residents of Mühlhausen. They recalled their one-time schoolteacher as a pleasant, if reserved, man. Far from being known as a sexual deviant (or even suspected of being one), he was remembered before the massacre as the very essence of respectability.

Added to these persecutory ideas were Wagner's beliefs about degeneration. Like many educated men at that time, he believed as a matter of fact that it was possible for families to carry hereditary taints that, generation by generation, became more destructive of intellectual, psychological and moral functioning. The degeneration theory was a confused conflation of half-understood genetics and misapplied ideas about evolution. Nevertheless, it grabbed the imagination of many leading writers and professionals in the latter half of the nineteenth century: notable examples included the psychiatrist Cesare Lombroso and the writer Émile Zola. The latter's magnificent Rougon-Macquart series of novels is a literary illustration of the theory interacting with social context in the succeeding generations of the two families who constitute his central characters. Under the influence of the degeneration ideology, Wagner became convinced he was a carrier of a degenerative trait that not only accounted for his father's alcoholism, his mother's moral turpitude and his uncle's madness, but also his own perverse sexuality – and which fatally predicted his children's inevitable decline into madness and moral decay.

The preoccupation with supposed persecution, the irrational fear of shameful exposure and the silly pseudoscience of degeneration combined to convince Wagner that he was not only trapped in a life of torment, but was doomed together with his entire family. Suicide was his escape. Wagner subsequently claimed the murders of his children were acts of compassion to save them from their fates. The killings at Mühlhausen were his revenge not only on his persecutors, but on a world that had never appreciated his genius. Finally, the dramatic nature of his actions and intended suicide were to guarantee him the literary fame he had previously been denied. Revenge, fame and death were to become the trifecta for our culture's *'amoks'*.

Still, Wagner's persecutory beliefs, however they preoccupied him, do not account for his carrying out a massacre. More significant is the fact that Wagner was a rigid man, obsessive by nature, and this gave him the commitment to plan and perpetrate such an event. The skewed value systems of the obsessive personality can create a rigid adherence to personal projects irrespective of the damage they may cause to the individual or those around them. Wagner's arrogance, grandiosity and self-absorption left him a stranger to even the modicum of fellow feeling that might have inhibited him from moving from fantasy to murderous action. His two Mauser ten-shot pistols provided the instruments to effect the massacre. Finally, Wagner's chronic pessimism, guilt and dejection allowed suicide to seem, for him, a rational choice. Depression, obsessiveness, grandiosity and resentment, in addition to delusions of persecution, make up the state of mind required for mass murder.

At the time, the case of Ernst Wagner briefly generated considerable media interest not only in his native Germany, but throughout the Western world. This event was not destined, however, to enter the public consciousness in the long term. Wagner attracted no would-be imitators. No fictional or documentary retelling of his story emerged for the general public. The notoriety of the event rapidly faded away.

Why was Wagner's influence so ephemeral compared with what was to come? Perhaps it was timing. Europe was rapidly descending into the great slaughter of 1914–18, and the news media had sensationalism enough without extending the life of the Wagner story. Perhaps it was the madness of Wagner: his was the crime of a psychotic, motivated by strange beliefs, alien and alienating. There was nothing here for others to identify with, because nobody else had a mind quite like that of the teacher from Stuttgart. Perhaps it was his failure to complete his project for murder-suicide that, as a result, left an image not of evil power with suicide as an ultimate act of revenge and self-aggrandisement, but of the humiliation and degradation of being exposed as a powerless lunatic. Perhaps it was simply that, at the time Wagner committed his crimes, there was no cultural gap waiting to be filled by a model for murder-suicide, even if he had managed to carry through his project to the intended self-immolation.

That Wagner left any mark even in the pages of psychiatric journals was only due to Gaupp, who wrote in detail and repeatedly about the case over the ensuing thirty years. Gaupp lived in the days before ethics committees, privacy laws and corporate lawyers to restrain the profession's ability to write about individual cases in a manner that could instruct and potentially improve medical practice. Within psychiatry, Wagner's case became, for a time, a bulwark against the spread of the ideology that all psychotic illnesses represented processes rooted in brain disease. Madness was not necessarily the product of some yet-to-be discovered abnormality of brain function: it could be the product of psychological and social stressors acting on someone whose personality and personal history left them especially vulnerable. As a result of Gaupp's efforts, we probably know more of Wagner, his world and why he carried out the massacre in 1913 than we know about all but a small number of subsequent mass killers of this type.

Wagner was psychotic. We now know, on the basis of large numbers of case analyses of lone-actor mass killers, that between 10 and 20 per cent are psychotic when they launch their attacks. Most have a disorder of a schizophrenic type, but just occasionally one will have a delusional disorder like Wagner.

There were just a handful of lone-actor massacres between Wagner's in 1913 and what was to become a seminal event: the massacre at the University of Texas in 1966. In January 1924, four women were killed and one seriously wounded during a shooting in Australia at Melbourne's Botanical Gardens. These victims were not together, nor known to each other, having been selected at random.

The rifle was found after the shooting, but not the murderer. A massive country-wide manhunt was launched for the owner of the gun. He was referred to in the press as a "mad gunman". A local psychiatrist gave an interview to the press describing exactly what kind of lunatic he was, despite never having seen him and knowing nothing of him beyond what little had appeared in the newspapers. Many a mental health professional has followed his example over the subsequent decades. In the event, he committed suicide a day or so later; his body was eventually found in a lake some 100 kilometres east of Melbourne.

The killer had served with distinction during the First World War, and according to his family he had never recovered from the experience. He had subsequently lived an isolated existence wandering around Australia and, for a period, the US, supporting himself as a casual labourer. Found among his possessions were books on mathematics and astronomy as well as a number of publications about guns. Nothing else was found that shed light on the massacre.

What was probably the first event of this kind in the US occurred in September 1949. A twenty-eight-year-old man shot and killed thirteen people and wounded three others in Camden, New Jersey. Like the Melbourne killer before him and the University of Texas shooter after him, he was a veteran, having served in the infantry during the Second World War. His rampage ended in a shootout with police but, though wounded, he survived to face trial. Psychiatrists assessing him noted his rigid, obsessive personality and "paranoid tendencies". He spoke at length about his resentment from previous humiliations and rejections, of which he retained both detailed memories and a minutely documented written record dating back to his childhood. The shootings were his last act of revenge, which he had planned in detail over the previous months. He was found to be insane at trial, on the basis of a dubious diagnosis of *dementia praecox* (schizophrenia), and lived out his life in a maximum-security mental hospital. This incident, like the Melbourne massacre before it, disappeared, leaving little trace in the collective memory.

The schoolmaster from Germany may claim precedence, but the full emergence of this type of mass murder as part of the West's social landscape did not occur until over fifty years later. In 1966, a twenty-five-year-old mature student dragged his gun cupboard up the last few flights to the top of the 90-metre-high granite tower of the University of Texas at Austin. There he shot the receptionist and went out onto the observation deck. A few moments later a group of sightseers attempted to enter the observation area, and he opened fire on them with a sawn-off shotgun, injuring four. He then jammed the door closed to prevent further disturbances and, having carefully organised his array of guns and some five hundred rounds of ammunition, began shooting down into the campus square below. He continued shooting for most of the next hour before a police team forced open the door of the observation deck and shot and killed him. When the police checked the houses of his wife and mother, they found them both dead.

What led this lone perpetrator to kill his mother, then his wife, and unleash a murderous rain of fire on his fellow students, killing fifteen people (including Karen Griffith [seventeen], Paul Sonntag [eighteen] and Dr Robert Boyar [thirty-three]) and seriously injuring another thirty? There were investigations by official committees and a multiplicity of journalists, and, perhaps most importantly, by television hosts and scriptwriters. The killer had been assessed by a psychiatrist at the student health service some months previously. Dr Maurice Heatly had found no evidence of a major mental disorder, but observed that the young man was a "naïve, muscular youth" who was self-centred and "oozing hostility", and who had mentioned going up the university tower to shoot people. (Such are the little disasters that can destroy a psychiatrist's reputation ...) His patient failed to attend a follow-up appointment and was not seen in consultation again.

At autopsy, a small brain tumour known as a hamartoma was discovered in the hypothalamic area. What role, if any, was played by the tumour was much debated, though the pathologist who performed the postmortem examination thought it was of no significance, given that small tumours of this type are not an uncommon finding at autopsy.

What was important for the long-term influence of this tragic event was both the nature and extent of the media coverage. The killer's name and photograph were everywhere. *The New York Times*, for example, devoted four columns on its front page to the massacre. He attained celebrity status, echoes of which are still to be found on the internet nearly sixty years after the event.

A further chapter in his elevation to an inspiration for lone mass killers occurred nine years later, when a TV docudrama was produced – an early example of this now-routine consequence of dramatic events. *The Deadly Tower*, starring Kurt Russell, provided an unintentionally heroic image of the killer. It begins with a voiceover intoning that "this senseless rampage" was "a crime against the whole of society". The film makes much of the perpetrator's obsession with guns, and is openly critical of the ease with which he was able to purchase an assault rifle with hundreds of rounds of ammunition. The bulk of the drama is taken up with the gun battle. Russell is given very few lines, but his handsome, brooding face is the film's dominant image. Before commencing the shooting, he dons a red bandana, a motif that will be repeated in the *Rambo* movies – hopefully not an intentional echo, but one that was noted by one of the lone mass killers I interviewed. The film portrays the University of Texas killer fighting off the combined firepower of the police, sheriff's department, FBI, Secret Service, National Guard and a multiplicity of self-appointed vigilantes who busily pepper the university tower with their hunting rifles. There is an attempt by the filmmakers to contrast the murdering character with a Mexican–American cop who is the embodiment of family and civic virtue. These good intentions fall short, and it is the monosyllabic Russell in his red bandana who steals the film. The explanation offered for the massacre is that the killer was driven mad by the brain tumour, which is incorrectly referred to as a "cancer".

The University of Texas killer became the face of death-dealing defiance, a vengeful mass killer who dies in a burst of public infamy. Graham Chester, on "motiveless random massacres" in his book *Berserk!*, concludes a detailed and perceptive account, noting:

> Like the heroes of popular movies such as *A Fistful of Dollars* and *For a Few Dollars More*, [the murderer] was, for the people of Austin on that hot August day, the nameless man, the stranger, the fast gun who takes the law into his own hands and stamps his will on a hostile world ... That the archetypal American hero parallels so closely the picture that gunmen have of themselves is surely not without significance, for in such a way, perhaps, do American Dreams become nightmares.

The Texas killer succeeded where the German schoolteacher failed, completing the plan for murder-suicide in a dramatic death atop the high tower. The young student was projected into the public consciousness not as a madman – misleading claims about brain cancer notwithstanding – but as a terrifying embodiment of evil. He was constructed as a threat to the very fabric of Middle America, as the face of hidden, suppressed, feared violence. His victims were predominately students, the future and the face of American success. He was an ex-soldier, a veteran of the Korean War, a marksman and an 'all-American boy' gone bad ... very, very bad.

Add to this a picture of violent despair, a dramatic public death, and above all celebrity, and you have a potential script for those who might find such an end desirable. There was not long to wait for the first imitator to emerge. In November 1966 an eighteen-year-old student at a college in Mesa, Arizona shot seven people, killing five, including Joyce Faye Sellers (twenty-seven), her three-year-old child Debra LaRae Sellers and Mary Margaret Olsen (eighteen). The killer claimed to have been inspired by his Austin predecessor.

In 2016, on the fiftieth anniversary of the massacre at the University of Texas, a remarkable documentary titled *Tower* was released, retelling the story of that terrible day. The film uses a combination of contemporary news footage and animation. The primary focus is on the victims and those caught up in the events. The killer makes no appearance other than as a vague shape high on the tower, and his name is mentioned only in passing. The film succeeds in conveying the appalling impact on those injured through actors reading from statements made immediately after the event, combined with recent interviews of some of the survivors. The extraordinary and skilful mixture of visual image and narrative brings home both the horror of that day and the courage and suffering of those involved. At the very end, the film gives a glimpse of the sequence of massacre after massacre that has occurred in the fifty years that have followed, and how little we have learned about guns, about disturbed and alienated young men and about how to present such tragedies in the media.

The Texas killer's name and his actions on that day have reverberated down the years. He has been a hero and a model for those who would become lone-actor mass killers themselves.

CHAPTER 4

A man on his way to commit a massacre

IN MANY WAYS, would-be lone mass killers – those who planned and attempted to perpetrate a massacre, but were stopped before the full realisation of their script – make for the most informative cases. They do not attract the media attention that surrounds figures such as the Port Arthur and Utøya killers, who succeeded and survived. In my experience of assessing this type of criminal, however, their accounts tend to be contaminated soon after the event by elements of self-justification, boasting and bravado. They also follow and read media reports, which can produce the odd experience for an assessing psychiatrist of hearing the speculation of journalists repeated back to you by the mass killer as part of their own narrative. There are also effects on the statements of those who knew these mass killers previously, as they adjust and edit their memories to emphasise certain details or reconstruct accounts to make sense of what has happened.

We now turn to a man who tried but failed to commit a massacre modelled closely on the 1966 University of Texas killings. S had been convicted in Australia of killing a security guard and attempting to kill two police officers. He claimed the initial murder, at first, to be accidental, despite evidence to the contrary. From the outset, however, he admitted that in the final exchange of gunfire with the police, he was attempting to provoke them into shooting him – but lost his nerve and fled. After he changed his plea to *guilty*, there seems to have been little attempt to re-examine his original story. The extent to which he had formulated a detailed plan for his murder-suicide was in some doubt at the time of his arrest and trial. Contemporary accounts varied widely. The trial received some media attention, but nothing like that which would have occurred had this case been regarded as a near-massacre. Following convictions for murder and attempted murder, S was sentenced to life in prison. It was only some years later that he acknowledged that he'd had the intention to perpetrate a massacre that would have forced the police to kill him.

When I first met him during his time in prison, he presented as an articulate man of well above-average intelligence. He was willing to provide an account of the events leading up to the shootings, and of his plans to commit a massacre. In the days immediately after his nineteenth birthday, he had resolved to kill himself. Life, he later reported, seemed to have become a pointless burden, with the future appearing to hold only further failure and humiliation. He had entertained violent fantasies for some years, like so many bullied and rejected youths, and before the incident he had nurtured an increasingly detailed daydream of climbing up to a high place and firing on people below until he himself was shot and killed by police. This fantasy had been informed, in part, by the 1966 University of Texas massacre, which he had learned about in his extensive reading on lone-actor massacres. Being killed was the central theme of the fantasy, but within the context of an attention-gripping drama.

He had owned a range of rifles, including a semi-automatic, and he was an experienced hunter and shooter. His actions over the week leading up to the attack were a mixture of impulsive and goal-directed. He drove around at night armed with his semi-automatic rifle. To test his resolve and nerve to carry out a massacre, he shot up a number of parked vehicles – but not before checking that there was no one around, and that his bullets would end up in a wall if they passed through the targets. On these nocturnal ramblings, he also walked over the route of the planned massacre, even ascending to the high vantage point from which he would be able to fire on the crowds below.

After failing to complete his plan to commit a massacre, he fled when faced with the imminent possibility of being shot and killed. He was captured later, after discarding his weapons. He attempted suicide on several occasions in prison on remand, and came very close to succeeding.

S grew up in a family in which expressions of affection had been limited. His parents' relatives lived in other parts of Australia, or overseas. His father was a self-contained man with few friends, and his mother was even more socially isolated: though she worked for years at the same job, she formed no friendships either there or in the neighbourhood where they lived. She developed a paranoid illness when he was about twelve years old, which led her to believe that her neighbours and coworkers were plotting against her and her family. The severity of her disorder fluctuated over subsequent years, but even at her best she remained suspicious and fearful of anyone outside of the family.

In childhood, the young S had difficulty socialising with his peers. His first language was not English, and he was markedly overweight: in primary and junior school, he seems to have attracted more than his fair share of bullying and exclusion as a result. In his teens, he found a small group of like-minded friends. He joined the Australian Army Cadets and subsequently the Army Reserve. Despite his intellectual abilities, he attained only modest success academically, though he could still have progressed to university. He chose, however, to leave school and look for work, a decision that separated him from his small group of friends. He started but soon gave up an apprenticeship; he then applied to join both the Army and the police, but was rejected by both on health grounds (which seem to have amounted to being too fat). He worked for a time as a casual labourer in a supermarket. Much of the year prior to the killing, he was unemployed and on the dole.

At home, he spent more and more time alone in his room, watching videos or reading. His only outings were to the gun club and to hunt with his father. His tastes in videos inclined to the vigilante and war genres. At his trial, the judge commented on his choice of movies, in particular *Rambo*, suggesting he was engaged in acting out a dangerous role of destruction copied from the videos and TV he watched. (S thought that was nonsense.) When his house was searched, a collection of gun magazines, largely from the US, were discovered together with multiple copies of *Soldier of Fortune*. He had books on the subject of serial killers as well as mass murderers.

The psychiatrists and psychologists who examined him after the killing all agreed he was depressed and suicidal. The depression was regarded as being of moderate to severe degree, with marked anxiety features. One expert speculated the shooting spree reflected a psychotic state acquired from his mother, in what is termed a *folie à deux*. This uncommon condition usually occurs when a psychotic individual draws a member of their family into sharing their delusional beliefs. This diagnosis had some slim basis in the facts, but seems, in retrospect, to have mostly been an exercise in clinical one-upmanship. As usual, a range of so-called personality disorders were diagnosed. Some psychiatrists favoured *schizoid*, some *antisocial*, some *borderline*, some a combination of all three; one alluded to sadistic personality traits as well. These diagnostic labels were, as ever, productive more of professional self-satisfaction than any enlightenment about the nature of the offender. Though S did not attract a diagnostic label of *obsessional*, several assessors commented on the accused's rigidity and tendency to excessive checking rituals and intrusive preoccupations.

S grew up in prison. Following a torrid couple of years marked by suicide attempts and futile conflicts with authority, he settled. Incarceration almost always harms prisoners in various ways. The prison population tends to comprise people drawn from less advantaged backgrounds, with many having experienced grossly disorganised and abusive childhoods. The majority are below average intelligence; even those of normal or superior intelligence are, for the most part, poorly educated. Such people usually lack the personal resources to cope with the pressures of confinement. They tend to lose what functional interpersonal and work skills they might have had, becoming absorbed into a prison culture marked by the use of intimidation and violence to maintain dominance. S was an exception – perhaps because of his intelligence or his supportive (albeit odd) family, who continued to visit, or because he was the kind of person who could resist pressure to conform to groups.

During his first couple of years in prison, the records noted that he had been involved in several fights with fellow prisoners. I wondered if this might have been therapeutic. Before the offences, he had been unwilling to stand up for himself in confrontations with either authority figures or peers who bullied and humiliated him. This torment had been the source of much of the resentment that plagued him. Now the fat, frightened youth had been transformed by regular workouts in the gym, and by the realisation that the worst had already happened and there was nothing left to fear. The fighting became less frequent and finally ceased, probably because he established a reputation as someone willing and able to defend himself.

Prior to his arrest, he had no involvement with drugs or alcohol. This abstemiousness continued in prison, saving him from entanglements with either gangs supplying drugs or prison authorities bent on punishing drug users. While in prison, he completed his education, obtaining a Bachelor of Arts degree. He attained a high level of physical fitness, shedding much of his excess weight. He even managed to find some like-minded friends. S came to be regarded as a model prisoner by the authorities, and even acquired status among fellow prisoners for his independence and willingness to provide helpful, informed advice on various problems.

When he was finally released on licence, he had to cope with the formidable challenges faced by all long-term prisoners upon returning to the community. He coped better than many, but not without setbacks and limitations. He was never able to allow casual acquaintanceships to develop into friendships – not just because they might find out about his past, but also because of his guilt and shame, irrespective of whether or not people knew what he had done. Finding paid employment was difficult both because of his criminal record and lack of a work history. In the end, he found part-time work that did not require contact with the public or much with other employees. He put his energies into his hobbies. His was a lonely and limited life. He did not become depressed again. At no point have his words or actions raised anxieties about violence, or even lesser forms of criminality. It is difficult to associate the somewhat shy, pleasant, articulate middle-aged man with his terrible actions of over thirty years ago.

S gave considerable thought over the years as to how he had finished up on a road that led to murder and could easily have culminated in a massacre. He believed his increasing absorption into a fantasy world dominated by violent retribution and heroic last stands had been an important influence. In the two years before the murder, he had lived as a hermit, with little or no contact with people outside the family (and even with them, communications were confined to the occasional exchange of mundane pleasantries). He lived in his head – and his head was full of anger and violence.

Looking back, he blamed himself for most of the problems. He believed his shyness, combined with an intense fear of failing, had paralysed him. These anxieties had prevented him from attempting to progress to university, to find a girlfriend, to take any initiative that might have allowed him re-entry into the world. He was able to recall how much time he felt he had also spent ruminating on the failures and humiliations of previous years. He now blamed himself for most of these problems, but admitted that he'd felt, at the time, that he had been unjustly treated. He shrugged off the possible influence of his mother's beliefs that the family was the object of persecution by malevolent forces.

He recalled how the plan to die in a final, violent act of retaliation against the world first emerged, and how it came to be his central focus. The weeks before the attack were taken up with imagining, preparing and elaborating the murderous plan, which would destroy the life of one man and rob S not only of many years of freedom, but also of the chance to ever live anything approaching a normal existence.

He was clear on why, in the end, he did not carry it through to its climax. It wasn't the actual shooting of the victim, which was accomplished by a rifle at a distance of twenty or thirty metres; it was when he removed the man's pistol that he was confronted with the awful reality of the death he had brought about. He had thought, up to that moment, that he'd been fully committed to a massacre, but his resolve was not sufficient to survive an up-close confrontation with his destruction of another person. The subsequent shootout had been intended to end in his own death, but even here his determination failed him and he fled. Retrospectively, he still perceived cowardice in his abandonment of the planned massacre and his own death, though he was more than thankful that he had not killed more people. I was inclined to a more generous interpretation that, in the end, he had broken through the world of fantasy in which he had been operating, and collided with the real-world effects of murder, which he recognised as terrible.

Suicidal, isolated, resentful, enraged, caught up in fantasies of heroic final showdowns and violent vengeance, rigid and obsessive, intensely interested in guns and things military and, finally, fixated on reports of previous lone-actor massacres: S ticked most of the boxes for what I regard as a profile typical of one type of lone mass killer. Perhaps, in the end, he was too decent and not sufficiently rigid to adhere to his plan, and not fully alienated from other people's humanity.

This case also demonstrates how much an individual can change over the years. We are not the people we were yesterday, however much our unreliable memories try to persuade us otherwise. Troubled people with what we can call for now, personality disorders, do tend to change more slowly in response to their shifting situations – but change they do. The only personality traits that frequently persist, largely unchanged, into later life are the obsessional and socially anxious ones. The more our personal and social situation changes, the more rapidly *we* change. Time, and maybe something we call *maturity*, inevitably alters who we are. The man who might have committed a massacre was not the man who left prison decades later.

CHAPTER 5

Dunblane

I HAVE CHOSEN to consider this tragedy in detail because of the extensive information available on its perpetrator. He is a grotesque, even in the ugly pantheon of mass killers. Anyone seeking an image of evil could have few better examples than this fat, balding nonentity carefully picking his way through crowds of terrified five- and six-year-old children and shooting randomly selected victims at point-blank range. What could lead anyone to shoot twenty-six little children and four teachers, leaving seventeen dead and many maimed for life? Among those he killed were Mellisa Currie (six), Megan Turner (five) and Kevin Hassell (six).

Following this massacre in Dunblane, Scotland, Britain's Houses of Parliament set up a joint public enquiry under a distinguished Scottish judge, William Douglas Cullen. The report inevitably creates more questions than it answers, but it does trace out many aspects of the killer's path to mass murder.

The Dunblane killer was born in 1952. His parents separated soon after his birth and he was adopted by his maternal grandparents. He grew up believing his mother was his sister – a far from rare event among working-class families at that time, for whom abortion was rarely an option. In effect, he became the only child of ageing parents, indulged and admired but kept at a distance. Of his childhood and development little seems to have emerged. He left school at sixteen to enter an apprenticeship as a draughtsman, which he never completed. As an adolescent and adult, he appears to have been odd, isolated and friendless.

He may have had a girlfriend in his teenage years, but this is uncertain. He is not known to have had intimate relationships with adult men or women, nor even casual sexual encounters, paid for or otherwise. All that is known of his sexuality is an intense preoccupation with photographs of eleven- and twelve-year-old boys in shorts or swimming trunks. When his house was searched after the murders, hundreds of photos and numerous videos were found containing images he had taken, over many years, of young boys. In the Cullen report are two documented episodes of him sexually molesting male children. There is also a mass of suggestive evidence that these two indecent assaults against boys were not isolated instances, but part of a pattern of surreptitious sexual exploitation of children.

The attempts, after the killings, to reconstruct his state of mind were frustrated by a dearth of relevant evidence. He was an isolate: he had acquaintances and neighbours, but no friends. He appears not to have confided in anyone. Casual conversations and superficial interactions had made up his social life for his entire adulthood. He had apparently never even attended a doctor's appointment, let alone one with a mental-health professional. Unlike some mass killers, he left no diaries or manifestos. However, he did leave behind a voluminous correspondence consisting almost exclusively of letters of complaint, threats of legal action and denials that he had ever molested boys.

The central activity in his life had been setting up and running boys' clubs. He established no fewer than fifteen between 1981 and 1996. Many were ephemeral, but several continued for years. These clubs often managed to obtain some level of official recognition, and usually met in halls controlled by schools and local authorities. To gain official sanction, he repeatedly misrepresented and even forged documents suggesting his clubs were supported and supervised by groups of respected citizens. He claimed influential sponsors up to and including Queen Elizabeth II, who, in reality – like his other supposed supporters – knew nothing of him and his activities. He devoted much of his time in the decade prior to the killings to founding and running his clubs, and defending them against criticism. Probably the time spent in these activities contributed to the failure of the 'home handyman' shop he ran between 1972 and 1985, and explains to some extent why, subsequently, he never worked in anything approaching regular employment.

After the Dunblane massacre, there was much soul-searching about how this man could have been allowed to continue for years running boys' clubs, despite so many concerns about his behaviour. Not only did he lack any relevant qualifications or genuine community support, he had been the subject of numerous complaints about his behaviour towards boys in his care dating back twenty years. In 1974 he had been removed from his role as a Scout troop leader and effectively banned from future involvement in the Scout movement. Dr Brian Fairgrieve, a senior figure in the Scottish Scouts, wrote at the time:

> While unable to give concrete evidence against this man ... I am far from happy about his having any association with scouts ... his personality displays evidence of a persecution complex combined with grandiose delusions of his own abilities ... as a doctor I am suspicious of his moral intentions towards boys.

How he managed to continue running boys' clubs tells us a great deal about him. He responded to any complaint or criticism with a barrage of denial and denunciation. He would immediately go on the offensive, accusing the complainant of lying, defaming him, victimising him; of every imaginable form of malfeasance. For example, his campaign against the Scout movement and those individuals within it he thought responsible for his exclusion would continue for more than two decades. Despite constant threats to take his accusers to court, though, he never actually litigated against anyone.

He did, however, manage to use the system repeatedly to precipitate a range of official enquiries into people he believed were accusing or investigating him. Two policemen who attempted to pursue him over accusations of acts of gross indecency with boys rapidly found themselves not the investigators, but the investigated. His complaints about them entangled the unfortunate officers in repeated enquiries into their behaviour.

(Nobody should underestimate the capacity of vexatious complainants to bring down the full weight of official bureaucracy on those they target. Complaints bureaus, ombudsmen's offices, registration boards, rights organisations and a multiplicity of commissioners for this, that and the other stand ready to hound citizens at the first letter of complaint. Organisations caught up in notions of due process and advocacy for the powerless rarely leave room for common sense, and too readily set the juggernauts of complaint investigation in motion. Though I am fortunate in never having been the object of an official complaint, I have spent many years advising organisations and individuals caught up in such litigation and trying to help patients who are ruining lives with abnormally persistent complaining.)

When the man who would become the Dunblane killer operated, in the 1980s and early 1990s, he had access only to a limited selection of agencies of accountability. (Today he would be able to generate even greater confusion for his enemies.) Even then, however, it was sufficient to protect him against those who might otherwise have prevented his operation of boys' clubs. His belligerent and self-righteous responses to any questioning of his behaviour may have been clever tactics; they were certainly effective. More likely, in my opinion, his reactions reflected primarily that combination of suspiciousness and grandiosity identified by Dr Fairgrieve. In his own mind, he *knew* he was right. Any criticism could only reflect malevolence and an attempt to destroy his good work. The reactions of the individuals and organisations to which he took his complaints would have reinforced his sense of rectitude, and probably created for him an illusion of supporters in high places. If he was like most vexatious complainants, he would have believed himself proved correct simply because agencies pursued his complaints at all.

He wrote at different times to the Queen, his MP and other members of the government. Such approaches almost always receive a *pro forma* reply of thanks for the letter, and an assurance that the contents will receive serious consideration. Into the bland politesse, chronic complainants read interest, support and, above all, confirmation of both their exaggerated notions of their own roles and of the importance of the cause they are pursuing. That nothing happens as a result of their letters in no way detracts from the comfort and encouragement they derive from the original response. Any subsequent communication that fails to support their complaints and accusations, for the most part, does not discomfit them either, but feeds their suspicions that other, even more powerful forces have intervened to turn their erstwhile supporters against them. When the future Dunblane killer's complaints were formally considered by various organisations – such as the police complaints body and the Scouts' central office – they were all judged, eventually, to be groundless.

His zeal for running boys' clubs involved an enormous expenditure of energy and resources. He literally devoted his life to these enterprises. The assumption that this was all a front to allow him to pursue his deviant sexual interests is, at best, a partial explanation. That he made money out of these activities is true, but he probably spent more on the clubs than he received back from the modest attendance fees. Certainly, at the time of his death, he was deeply in debt.

The accounts from boys who came to his clubs suggest that he revelled in running a regimented programme with activities in which he was always the leader. Although exercises that involved lots of small boys running around in black trunks without shirts or in singlets impress themselves vividly on the imagination, most of their time seems to have been spent in activities modelled on those of Scout troops. The major difference was the extent to which this man felt the need to impose his moment-to-moment control. The admiration of the young, and a realm in which he could be the unassailable dominant figure, were important motivations for running the clubs. Given his total failure to establish himself in any effective adult roles, there might also have been an element of nostalgic return to an idealised childhood where he was the unchallenged centre of admiring attention. Whatever the balance of satisfactions he extracted from operating the clubs, they added up to the core of his existence. The only other subject that seems to have engaged his interests in the last few years of his life was guns.

This eventual killer of small children was first granted a firearms licence in 1977. He renewed and modified it repeatedly over the years, allowing him to legally accumulate a range of weapons and a substantial store of ammunition. He joined several gun clubs. Though they provided a venue for him to develop his shooting skills, they did not constitute an environment in which shared interests could produce social interactions, let alone friendships. Members of the gun clubs who were interviewed after the massacre were almost uniformly of the opinion that the killer was a loner who could not conform to the most basic club rules. One member described him as "a right weirdo who talked about guns as if they were babies".

He left behind no statement explaining why he had committed himself to this peculiarly horrible form of murder-suicide. We know it was no impulsive act of despair, as there is ample evidence of his acquiring the instruments for mass murder over previous months, and of his enquiring about, and visiting, the school in the weeks leading up to the attack.

Many years later, when I was involved with a group of colleagues carrying out research into people who stalk, threaten, intrude upon or launch attacks on members of the British Royal Family, two letters from him to the Queen surfaced. The letters, for the most part, petitioned for royal support both for his clubs and for protection against the attacks of officialdom in general and the Scout movement in particular. In the knowledge of what was to occur, the final paragraph of his last letter to the Queen – posted some days before the massacre – takes on a chilling quality: "I turn to you as a last resort and am appealing for your support that I may be able to regain my self-esteem in society."

Research since this time has shown that the phrase *a last resort* in letters to heads of state and political leaders should be regarded as a warning that the correspondent is at risk of taking action likely to harm themselves or others. The individual indicating they no longer see any other option should always raise the suspicion of possible suicide or violence to others. This is particularly the case in chronic complainants and the querulous, such as the Dunblane killer.

The Cullen report found no evidence that he had told anyone about his murderous plans or uttered threats to kill. It states that this massacre was meticulously planned and prepared. Why he had wished to end his own life is clear: he was facing financial ruin. The last of his boys' clubs was at imminent risk of closure, and the chances of his ever obtaining the necessary support for any new venture were remote. The possibility of prosecution for child molesting still hung over him. He was a friendless, middle-aged man who was losing everything he held of value, and who had no obvious prospect of creating a new life for himself.

To the extent that the observations of neighbours and casual acquaintances can be relied upon, he was not obviously depressed. There is ample evidence that he was, to say the least, a suspicious man convinced he was the victim of repeated injustices and campaigns of vilification. His grandiosity may well have fed his resentment against a world that had failed to recognise his genius. He is repeatedly described as rigid and obsessive, qualities that, as we have seen, make it possible to carry out projects of mass murder. But disappointed, egotistical, isolated and rigid men are ten a penny. Such people may resort, on occasion, to suicide, but not the mass murder of little children.

Distinguished experts from psychology and psychiatry were called upon by the committee of enquiry to try to explain his motives and state of mind at the time. Their reports were stronger on what he was *not* rather than on what might have driven his behaviour. He was not seriously mentally ill; on that the experts were firm in their opinions. This man, they made clear, was not a man driven by the internal demons of delusion. In the event, the experts opted for speculation, positing that he had a sadistic personality. Such views seem to rest entirely on theories plucked from the literature rather than being grounded in what was actually known about the man. Looking back decades later, unconstrained by the pressures that must have weighed on the enquiry and its experts, it seems that at least the possibility of a paranoid illness should have been entertained, given his mixture of self-importance, vexatiousness and persecutory ideas.

The Dunblane killer did not survive to answer questions; and unlike so many examples of this type of mass killer, he left no testament to glorify his actions. A suspicious, oversensitive, rigid, querulous isolate, he functioned too well to have had chronic, untreated schizophrenia. Other than his prickly pomposity and energetic pursuit of boys' clubs and boys, there is nothing to suggest a manic illness. He, like most people, almost certainly experienced depression in the form of periods of lowered mood and pessimism – but there are no accounts suggesting extended periods of profound mood disorder. From the perspective of most mental health professionals today, he thus had no psychotic or serious mental disorder. Psychiatrists of previous generations might have identified a paranoid illness, but they were not constrained by the current prevailing psychiatric ideology, which identifies psychosis entirely with a process reflecting changes in the brain, the nature of which are the subject of much speculation but little knowledge. That type of illness, this man did not have.

What he *did* have were those characteristics to be found in many of the perpetrators of single-actor massacres. He was, like them, a loner caught up in the collapse of his ambitions and battered by losses varying from financial to abandonment. He shared their despair to the point of becoming suicidal. Like so many who commit solo massacres, he was enraged at a world that had not only failed to recognise his genius, but had gone out of its way to subject him to rejection and humiliation. He was resentful and rigidly obsessive, as are many of the others.

In his case we know nothing about his fantasy life, though some might be inclined to construct notions of his sexual imaginings from the enormous number of photos of little boys in their navy-blue shorts and plimsolls, which passed in those long-off days for sporting apparel. On this evidence he seems to me to have been burdened with a curiously constrained sexuality redolent of the 'fetishistic', at least as much as the 'paedophilic'. We do know that he shared the intense fascination with guns found in so many mass killers.

In my opinion, the Dunblane killer differed from most, though not all, lone perpetrators of massacres in that he was almost certainly deluded at the time he planned and executed his terrible crimes. Delusional disorders emerge gradually out of the interaction between particular personality traits and the circumstances of the subject's progress through life – or, more precisely, their *failure* to progress through the life they had conceived for themselves. The Dunblane killer believed he had a gift for communicating with young people and outstanding abilities as an organiser of boys' clubs at least on a par with the Scout movement, if not superior to it. There is ample evidence of his bombastic self-promotion and grossly exaggerated claims about his experience and knowledge of running these clubs. In his various letters of complaint and petitions, he demonstrates repeatedly that he knew he was right and that those who arraigned against him were malevolent conspirators.

Like Wagner, the deluded headmaster from Germany, he had a sexual secret. What both men seem to have feared most was their hidden sexuality being revealed by those bent on frustrating their worldly ambitions. Wagner was plagued by guilt and shame about an instance of bestiality. Was the Dunblane killer also ashamed of his hidden desires and forbidden sexuality? We do not know; but we do know he was terrified of having his sexual proclivities publicly exposed.

At what point do exaggerated notions of personal superiority and beliefs that you are surrounded not just by ill will but active persecution cease to be personality factors and become delusions? Psychiatry, both in theory and in practice, has always had problems pinning down this point of transition. An intermediate stage was even invented to place between the domains of personality and delusion, called *overvalued ideas* or *delusion-like ideas*. The main function of these "overvalued ideas" seems to me to be to allow mental-health professionals not only to avoid making a decision about whether or not a person is deluded but, far more importantly, to disclaim any responsibility for treating and managing them. Just words – does it really matter? Not in the case of the Dunblane killer, because he was never psychiatrically assessed and never placed himself in a situation where he might have been compelled to undergo such an assessment.

In other cases, it has most certainly mattered. I have come across killers with delusional disorders who had been seen by psychiatrists and were not recognised as psychotic. They were not provided with any treatment, or even supervision. In a number of cases, the only people who seem to have failed to recognise that the killer was psychotic were psychiatrists. In one case a man had, over a three-year period, been taken on two occasions by the police for psychiatric assessment because they thought he was clearly psychotic; and on a further occasion he was referred by an orthopaedic surgeon to his mental-health colleagues because the man had become "obviously deluded" while being treated on the ward following a road traffic accident. The man's wife, his mother and his only friend all told the mental-health services at various times that he was deluded, and that he had ceased to function on almost every level. All three psychiatrists who assessed him discharged him without treatment or follow-up, because they considered he was either a paranoid personality or that he had "overvalued ideas". He killed his only child, then himself.

How can such potentially fatal mistakes be reduced? Listening for long enough to what the patients have to say is the first step. The second step is taking proper note of their behaviour, and of the impact it has on their lives and the lives of others around them. Those in the grip of a delusional disorder lose all sense of proportion, and eventually even their own lives and the lives of others come to seem less important than vindication and victory.

We do not have a record of the Dunblane killer explaining his side of the story, but we do know about his behaviour and its impact on his life. He may always have been somewhat marginal in his social and economic adjustments, but in the years leading up to the massacre his functioning deteriorated rapidly. His debts escalated, his mortgage remained unpaid and what little contact he had with other adults virtually ceased.

He had, for many years, devoted more time to his boys' clubs than was wise from an economic standpoint. In the preceding few years, however, it was his pursuit of complaints and his battle to justify and promote himself and his clubs that consumed almost all his energies. His life appears to have become dominated by his quest for his notion of justice, and for vindication of his claims to being an exemplary group leader innocent of all sexual misconduct. His grandiosity, his beliefs in unjust persecution and his need for vindication were apparent in those behaviours, which finally collapsed the financial and social framework on which his life depended. Without his account we cannot be sure; but to me it appears to be delusion, or *feels* like it: a delusion that pushed him across that line from suicidal despair to mass murder.

He was an interloper who entered a school to kill. However, most school shootings are not perpetrated by murderous strangers who bring their guns onto school property, but by murderous pupils.

CHAPTER 6

An act of madness?

J WAS A postgraduate university student facing two charges of murder and multiple charges of attempted murder. He had taken two loaded pistols to his regular seminar. Accounts differ as to exactly what occurred, as would be expected from a group of people who had gone through a terrifying experience in which some were injured and all faced imminent death. It would seem that J arrived late. By the time he entered the room, the lecturer and all the other students were already seated and discussing the topic of the day. Standing in the doorway, J took out the guns and began shooting. It is not known for certain if he targeted specific people, fired at random or both. The toll of dead and injured would have been even higher had two brave men not run at him and, despite one being shot, managed to overpower J and end the massacre.

J shared many of the characteristics of so many other lone-actor mass killers. Here was another young male, socially isolated, intensely resentful of the injustices and humiliations to which he believed he had been subjected, with an exaggerated opinion of his abilities; he had recently experienced failures that put his plans in jeopardy; and he was despairing, suicidal and – last but not least – gun-obsessed. The way he differed from most other lone actors is that he had a history of diagnosis and treatment for a schizophrenic disorder.

J had reported persecutory delusions and auditory hallucinations during a previous episode of illness some four years earlier. At that time, he had been admitted to a psychiatric hospital for several months and treated with antipsychotic medication. Following discharge, attempts had been made to treat him as an outpatient, but this stopped when he moved to Australia. He had had no contact with the Australian mental-health services in the two years before the shootings. He denied any recent psychotic experiences when examined after the killings.

He was not an easy man to interview, partly because he was well aware that disclosing unusual experiences and beliefs would lead to his being placed once more on antipsychotic medication. This was an outcome that he wished to avoid, even at the cost of being convicted on two murder charges and multiple attempted-murder charges.

J was the only child of a professional couple, and had had a privileged home background. His mother's account suggested normal early development, and she knew of no difficulties in his preschool placements. In primary and secondary school he progressed well academically, which seems to have been a high priority for his parents. He may or may not have had problems in primary school, but his mother acknowledged that he was a loner at secondary school who avoided participation in sports and other group activities. At home he spent more and more time alone in his room as the years passed. He managed to obtain entry to university, but continued to live at home with no signs of developing much in the way of friends and acquaintances. He did manage to join the university's Army cadet force, though little is known of his functioning in this context. One thing we do know is he developed a passion for guns.

University staff in his home country, China, became concerned about his mental state at the beginning of his final year. He had made a number of complaints about his treatment in class, and about being in danger from fellow students. When seen by student-health services, he reported hearing voices in addition to delusions of being persecuted. He was hospitalised and started on antipsychotics. After a long admission period, he returned to his parental home while continuing to take medication and checking in with a mental-health team. He eventually returned to university and was finally awarded a degree. His hope was to proceed to a postgraduate qualification, but he could not obtain a place in any Chinese university, possibly because of his mental-health history. It was decided that his parents would finance his pursuit of a Master's degree in Australia. He secured a place as a full fee-paying student. He initially came to Australia with his mother as a support person. No contact was made with the local mental-health services, and no attempt was made to inform the university about his mental-health history.

In Australia, there seem to have been problems from the outset of the course, with his performance in written assignments and especially participation in seminars. These issues were initially attributed to a combination of language difficulties and shyness. J managed to stumble through the first year, but in the second, his performance deteriorated further, and the frequency of his complaints increased – both about the teaching and his fellow students.

Before the attack, one of the lecturers attempted to be helpful by initiating a discussion with him about whether or not this was the course best suited to his needs. J responded with an angry diatribe about how badly he was being treated.

J did not seem to have developed even superficial relationships with fellow students, either in his course or with various university groups, including those with members from similar language and cultural backgrounds. There was a report that he had joined a gun club, though no details are known. What we do know is that he obtained a number of guns, including two handguns. Possession of handguns is prohibited in Australia unless the person fulfils the strict licensing criteria. J had no such permission, and had procured the guns on the black market.

Of all the lone-actor killers I have had the opportunity to examine, this man was the least forthcoming about his thoughts and feelings. His schizophrenic psychosis alone does not explain how resistant he was to all attempts to explore his internal world. Most people with psychotic illnesses will speak about their experiences, given the opportunity and the time in which to feel sufficiently safe. The main bar to communication is usually not their unwillingness to describe what has been happening but their difficulty in finding words to adequately capture the strangeness of some of these occurrences.

Even those made intensely suspicious by their delusional beliefs will usually become more open as the grip of the psychosis loosens, either with treatment or simply the passage of time. J, even after years on antipsychotic medication, continued to offer little beyond denials of any experiences that might suggest he was psychotic – denials that were difficult to square with some of his observable behaviours. He would, for example, occasionally accuse other patients or staff, angrily, of talking about him and insulting him. There were also times when he would yell at the television, apparently upset by the content of programmes about which, for others, there was difficulty in seeing any connection to him or his situation.

When I sat with him, he would sometimes say something out of the blue that revealed some internal dialogue, hinting at strange happenings and experiences. These brief, fractured discourses would end as suddenly as they had begun. Attempts to clarify what he had said and its meaning were always met with disavowals and denials that he had said anything. Eugen Bleuler, the great Swiss psychiatrist who coined the term *schizophrenia*, described such episodes in some of his patients. He likened them to standing for hours before a silent, apparently vacant house when suddenly a curtain is partially drawn aside to reveal a glimpse of a party in full swing; then the curtain falls back to return the house to its previous state.

J did say at one point that he'd expected to be killed on the day of the shootings, but did not clarify whether this was what he wanted to occur, or a risk he was prepared to accept.

The extent of this man's alienation from the feelings and attitudes of most human beings was illustrated by an incident over a pair of jeans. When he was being managed on a psychiatric unit, an observant nurse noticed he had been wearing the same obviously dirty, stained jeans for several weeks. This was in dramatic contrast to his usual meticulous cleanliness. When she asked him about the jeans, he ignored the question and walked away, which was often his response to an enquiry.

Curious, the nurse looked through the records for the origin of the jeans. She discovered that they had been in a collection of personal possessions returned to J by the police a couple of months earlier, after the conclusion of his trial. They were the jeans he had been wearing when he had committed the massacre. In the police docket, the garment was described as bloodstained.

The unit staff became understandably upset by this discovery. I was asked what they should do, and suggested that the following evening, when he was in bed, the jeans be removed and destroyed. One of the staff asked if they were allowed to do that. My response was to the effect that I neither knew nor cared. The jeans were removed that night by relieved staff, and a new pair of clean jeans without sinister provenance was substituted. J would never talk about his lost jeans, other than occasionally demanding that his property, unspecified, be returned. Given his usual dedication to the obsessive washing of his clothes it was difficult to avoid the suspicion that this souvenir of his killings had provided some awful satisfaction that outweighed even his obsessive cleanliness.

It is probable that at least 30–40 per cent of those who commit lone mass attacks have had contact with mental-health services earlier in their lives. In many of the cases from the US that is all the detail we know, because of the reluctance of psychiatrists and psychologists to release records even to official enquiries. It is reasonable to assume that most, if not all, of those killers who survive their massacre to face trial have been psychiatrically evaluated. The results of such evaluations are occasionally revealed during the trial, but this is by no means always the case. In other parts of the world, in the enquiries and trials that follow such massacres, mental-health histories and post-offence evaluations are more often made public – sometimes in detail, though more often in a précis of the main findings. Information about the potential role of mental disorders in lone mass killers is therefore patchy, but sufficient for us to draw some tentative conclusions.

The question of psychosis is relevant to any enquiry into the cause and prevention of lone mass killings. To murder strangers with the expectation of dying among your victims is surely an act of madness. The act is mad in the everyday sense of that word; but are the perpetrators mad in the sense of being afflicted by a severe mental illness?

Some of the lone mass killers labelled "schizophrenic" may not have had any such disorder. The Camden, New Jersey killer of 1949, who committed what was probably the first lone-actor massacre in the US, was found at his trial to be insane on the basis of a diagnosis of *dementia praecox*, an earlier term for schizophrenia. The grounds for making this determination were, however, dubious at best. The Utøya killer was diagnosed as having schizophrenia by two court-appointed psychiatrists, though this diagnosis was opposed by two other psychiatrists. A psychiatrist local to the Aramoana shooter publicly announced that he had schizophrenia, though she had never seen the man. This led subsequently to his being included among schizophrenic mass shooters in several publications. There was, in fact, no evidence for the diagnosis, and ample information to the contrary, including a previous psychiatric evaluation that virtually ruled out psychosis. Conversely, there are many other cases in which psychosis may well have been present, but was either dismissed or not considered in the reports and enquiries that followed the massacres.

Often those who perpetrate lone-actor attacks go out of their way to deny that they are in any way mentally disturbed. Theirs, they claim, is a righteous act, not the product of any personal psychopathology. The Utøya killer was enraged when the first psychiatric evaluations suggested he was mentally ill rather than a hero of the resistance to "cultural Marxism". The Virginia Tech killer, in his recordings and manifesto, denied that he had ever been mentally ill, and emphasised the essentially rational basis for his acts.

The perpetrators whom I have assessed all denied that their actions had been in any way a reflection of personal psychopathology. The one who did have schizophrenia made great efforts to avoid revealing the thoughts and experiences he rightly suspected would point to his being psychotic. Until the very last minute, this man resisted a defence predicated on his being mentally ill. Another man I evaluated following his attack on an abortion clinic (in which one person was killed and others injured) not only went to great lengths to hide his religious and grandiose delusions but, when they were revealed, refused to allow his legal team to use the resultant psychiatric reports in his defence. He wanted to be a righteous martyr suffering for a great cause, and the court obliged him with a lengthy prison sentence.

It is a mistake to believe that lone-actor killers, whether terrorist-inspired or not, seek to avoid responsibility for their actions. Quite the opposite: most prefer to glory in their achievements, or to lament their failure to complete their murderous endeavour.

One feature of the typical lone mass shooter that fits poorly with the popular idea of a psychotic killer is the careful planning and the coldly efficient manner in which these killings are so often achieved. In fact, psychotic people who kill are more, not less, likely to have planned and prepared their murderous attack by comparison with other homicide offenders. In a study with Deb Bennett – both a serving police officer in Australia and a psychologist with whom I worked – covering over 400 homicides, we found that the thirty-odd killings perpetrated by a murderer with a schizophrenic illness were more, not less likely, to have been planned beforehand and to have been motivated by carefully considered, even if sometimes bizarre beliefs. The psychotic killers in some cases had been waiting quite long periods for an auspicious opportunity. In contrast, non-psychotic homicide offenders were more likely to act impulsively in a highly aroused state, not only having never planned but never even considered killing their victim on this occasion, or anyone else on any other occasion. So, there is no reason to assume that a psychotic person cannot plan, prepare and carry out homicidal violence.

There are also factors that could be considered inherent to some forms of schizophrenic disorder that might predispose to murderous or otherwise violent behaviours. The most obvious is *delusion*. There are types of delusion that drive those in their grip to violence, such as the delusions of infidelity found in pathological jealousy. In contrast, those troubled by persecutory delusions usually attempt to withdraw from other people and hide from those they believe are plotting against them. Delusions of persecution only rarely motivate the sufferers to confront their supposed antagonists, let alone retaliate with violence. This being said, because persecutory delusions are by far the most common type, even though they less commonly lead to attacks they still make up the majority of the delusions that precipitate violent acts.

Only a tiny proportion of killers who are deluded ever threaten, let alone attack, anyone. In the small minority who do launch attacks, there are almost always other forces at work, not just delusions.

If not delusions, what else contributes to explaining the higher rates of psychotic people among those who perpetrate homicidal violence, including lone-actor massacres? Those with psychotic disorders who resort to violence often share the same social and personal problems that might predispose to violence any member of the community. The difference is in the frequency with which these are present in the schizophrenias. In other words, perpetrators of lone mass killings who have a psychotic disorder look for the most part just like mass killers who are not psychotic.

CHAPTER 7

Massacres in schools and universities

THERE IS SOMETHING particularly shocking about a schoolboy taking a gun to school to kill and maim fellow students. If anything, the horrific nature of such events is amplified by the targets being chosen at random rather than because they are individuals against whom the shooter bears a grudge. The attack is on the whole school, and often, as with other lone-perpetrator massacres, intended to be an act of revenge against all of society. The seminal event in the rise and rise of the lone-actor massacre was the University of Texas shooting in 1966. Since then, in the US, school and campus shootings continue to make up about a third of such events. They have also occurred, at a lower rate, in Canada, the UK, Europe, South America and Australia.

My only experience of evaluating a potential adolescent mass killer involved a thirteen-year-old boy. Having first shot his mother, he walked a few hundred yards to a commercial street where he began firing on people at random, injuring several. The event was brought to an end by a policeman who tackled him while he was attempting to reload. The shooting of the mother had occurred when she'd tried to prevent him from leaving the house with the rifle. This was almost certainly accidental, and what followed can be viewed as an act of despair. Evidence emerged subsequently, however, from both the boy and fellow pupils, that he had talked of committing a massacre at his school. As usual in such situations, most of his classmates did not take the threat seriously, but one boy in particular had kept asking him when he was going to bring his gun to school and carry out his promise to shoot the headmaster and teachers.

The actual shooting did not, in the end, involve the school. Whether or not the fact that he had been entertaining fantasies of shooting people played a role was difficult to establish. The boy denied it. He also denied that he had in any way been influenced by a massacre some weeks previously, which had received enormous publicity. Again, evidence gathered subsequently by the police indicated he had talked with schoolmates about this massacre, even suggesting that he would act in a like manner. I suspect this rather complex interaction between pre-existing fantasies and vague hints with a deeply distressing provocation were important determinants of the eventual tragedy. In this case, as in so many others, the availability of guns in the home and the boy's fascination with weapons, shooting and things military contributed to an environment out of which such horrific behaviour could emerge.

The massacre at the Columbine High School in Columbine, Ohio, in April 1999 left fifteen dead, including the two killers, with over twenty more injured. Among the dead were Rachel Scott, Corey Depooter and John Tomlin, all seventeen years of age. The official report was published in 2001. It is, in many ways, a disappointing document, particularly when compared to the Cullen report prepared for the UK government following the massacre at Dunblane. The differences are in part attributable to the powers available to the two enquiries. Cullen had all the powers of a British royal commission. No documents were closed to his enquiry, and no potential witness could decline to be examined under oath. In contrast, the Columbine enquiry could not even force the local Jefferson County Sheriff's Office to hand over its documents, nor could it compel witnesses to attend and answer questions. The enquiry was even denied full access to the perpetrators' medical records.

Sadly, the priority for the police, medical practitioners and some witnesses seems to have been to protect themselves from being held liable in a potential lawsuit. As a result, the enquiry into Columbine, though providing considerable information about what occurred, is frustrating for those who wish to understand the *why* rather than the *how* of the tragedy. The enquiry did have access to the journals and occasional writings of the two boys who committed the massacre, A and B. These are still accessible on the internet. Also accessible is the video the boys prepared immediately before the attack. Most revealing in many ways, and heartrending, is the book *A Mother's Reckoning: Living in the Aftermath of Tragedy*, by the mother of one of the attackers.

Columbine is a secondary school of some 2,000 pupils on the southern outskirts of Denver, Colorado, serving a reasonably prosperous neighbourhood. It has a number of famous alumni, including the creators of the brilliant, quirky TV series *South Park*. There are two narratives as to why the tragedy happened; the first is drawn from what was observed by others before the attack, and the second, from the writings left behind by the two perpetrators.

A and B were considered by their teachers to have above-average abilities. They were not believed by school authorities to have been singled out for bullying, nor to have been prone to bullying others. A had been treated for depression and had been placed on antidepressants, which the postmortem blood samples demonstrated he was still taking. B, it was noted, had been withdrawn and sad in the weeks before the killings, but there is no record of any formal mental-health assessment. Both boys had been convicted in January 1998 of breaking into a tradesman's van and stealing various electrical goods. Whether the thefts were connected to their bomb-making efforts is not clarified in the report. Following conviction for these offences, they were placed on what amounted to a good-behaviour bond and compelled to attend a youth justice centre for counselling.

A was the son of a career Air Force officer, and his early years had been marked by moves occasioned by his father's various postings.

The family had, however, been settled in the Jefferson County area throughout his secondary-school years. B also came from a privileged and stable family background. Both sets of parents had been aware to some extent that their sons were becoming increasingly withdrawn and apparently unhappy in the months before the killings. A's parents had initiated a referral to a local mental-health professional, who had prescribed an antidepressant. The details of the assessment and subsequent psychological management do not seem to be available. A's hopes of following in his father's footsteps by entering the military received a setback shortly before the killings when his application to the Marine Corps was rejected on health grounds. The basis for this decision was Harris's use of antidepressants, as well as the fact that he had a minor structural anomaly of his sternum, *pectus excavatum*, which is usually of cosmetic rather than functional significance.

A and B were keen shooters with access to a variety of guns. They had even made a film of themselves target shooting. In addition, they purchased pump-action shotguns and a 9mm semi-automatic carbine at a Denver gun show before the massacre. On the day of the killings, they also had a semi-automatic pistol. They told fellow pupils about having these weapons, and they had also talked at school of their bomb-making efforts. Neither any of the teachers nor the parents were informed about these revelations. The friendship between the boys had developed a couple of years previously, and had progressed to the point where they became an exclusive duo, spending much of their time together, largely isolated from peers and even from family members.

To the outside world, the boys appeared to be a couple of close friends sharing interests in computers and an enthusiasm for guns and shooting. I would hazard a guess that the parents were probably reassured that each had such a good friend. To their peers they appeared standoffish, affecting an air of superiority. Neither boy had a girlfriend at the time of the massacre, but in the past both had dated. The parents and teachers were aware that the boys were somewhat troubled and not performing academically and socially at the level that would have been predicted from their functioning at earlier stages in their schooling. The theft from the electrician's van had raised concerns, but the boys' explanation that it was an impulsive prank seems to have been accepted.

In the weeks preceding the attack, A had posted death threats on his web page, leading to questions being asked and to some kind of psychiatric assessment, the details of which remain obscure. Whatever the conclusions may have been, no action was taken. In the context of the local culture, the interest in guns and shooting was not unusual. Had the purchases of semi-automatics and pump-action shotguns by a depressed teenager been known, perhaps concerns might have been raised – but then again, maybe not. In short, A and B appeared to be like many other reasonably bright adolescents from privileged backgrounds struggling with the transition to more adult roles.

The boys' web-page entries, and the writings found after the massacre, paint an entirely different picture. The official report characterised A's web page as "seething with suicidal anger and rage". As early as 1997, A was confiding to his journal both that he was contemplating suicide and that he wanted to go on a killing spree. One entry contains the words: *I am an outcast and everyone is conspiring against me.* On another occasion he wrote: *I hate you people for leaving me out of so many fun things.* B, in his writings, noted: *My wrath for the January incident* [the prosecution for theft] *will be godlike.*

Alongside the anger at being rejected and ignored were statements about their assumed superiority to those around them, including: *we have evolved above you humans.* There are also references to the works of Friedrich Nietzsche, some of which propose the concept of the *Übermensch*, unconstrained by the moral principles of the common herd. This interest in Nietzsche is reminiscent of the infamous case of Nathan Leopold and Richard Loeb, two students from Chicago who, in 1924, kidnapped and murdered a fourteen-year-old boy to prove their intellectual and moral superiority.

The boys' writings demonstrate the extent of the planning and preparation that preceded the actual attack – or, in words of the report, "they accumulated data and lethal instrumentalities over many months".

Hindsight can, as usual, find signs pointing to the eventual tragedy. The fact of the massacre endowed apparently insignificant events with a sinister meaning. Retrospection allows connections to be made between occurrences that, at the time, nobody had been in a position to see. Even if a competent evaluation had followed the revelation of the death threats on the website, without the boys' cooperation or knowledge of their writings and preparations it would have been difficult to predict the possibility of a massacre. The defensiveness of some of the professionals, and the reluctance to reveal to the enquiry what they knew or ought to have known, makes it difficult to determine whether or not there was any chance that this massacre could have been foreseen.

This is not to say that, even in the absence of any suspicion of what was to come, nothing could have been done to reduce the chances of such a tragedy. One lost opportunity for potential intervention was a more effective management of the state of despair and potential for suicide that were apparent in B, at least. That he had fallen under the influence of A may well have been mistaken for the development of a positive and supportive relationship. Post-massacre, this now looks more like a dynamic in which one half of an isolated pair has radicalised the other. (The problem here is that, though A was the dominant figure, it was B who more closely resembled the typical lone-actor mass killer.) Something might also have been done about the pair's ability to accumulate an arsenal of military armaments. And perhaps responding more proactively to the decline in performance and the increasing isolation of these two previously bright and able boys might have made a difference. These failures, if failures they be, stem less from any individual's deficiencies and more from the limited capacity of our society to tackle such issues.

*

The Sandy Hook massacre in Newtown, Connecticut, is as terrible as that in Dunblane. On 14 December 2012 a twenty-one-year-old man shot and killed his mother. He then travelled the short distance to Sandy Hook Elementary School, where he shot and killed twenty little children and seven adults, leaving two others seriously wounded. Among those killed were Olivia Engel, Emilie Parker and Noah Posner, each six years old. The horrific attack ended when the man turned his weapon on himself.

The killer had attended Sandy Hook between 1990 and 2003, but had experienced no known contact with the school or its staff since. He was the younger of two boys; his parents had separated when he was nine, and he alone remained with his mother. He had undergone a troubled childhood, and was assessed by various mental-health professionals over the period of his schooling. He had shown some difficulties from early childhood: he was slow to develop physical dexterity, remaining throughout his life awkward and poorly coordinated. His social development was slow, and he continued to be socially inept at best. Nothing is known about his sexual development beyond his never having had either a girlfriend or boyfriend.

He developed ritualised behaviours such as repeatedly touching, or carefully avoiding touching, particular objects. Such behaviour was accompanied by obsessive attitudes towards matters such as the preparation and consumption of food. He was also obsessive about cleanliness, which involved an excessive fear of dirt and contamination leading to repeated hand-washing. with frequent demands for changes of clothes. These were obsessive, not obsessional, phenomena. The key difference is that the obsessional recognises that their fears and compulsions are irrational, or at least irrationally insistent, and consequentially tries – often unsuccessfully – to resist their performance. The obsessive, by contrast, sees these fears and compulsions as perfectly reasonable, and therefore does not resist their performance.

The combination of extreme social difficulties with interpersonal deficits, marked obsessive traits and poor physical coordination led several professionals to conclude that the future killer had autism spectrum disorder (then also labelled "Asperger's syndrome"). He also appears to have had an eating disorder, and was seriously underweight at the time of the massacre.

There were various attempts at managing his problems, but he was resistant to all such efforts. He was prescribed antidepressants at one point, but these were discontinued by his mother because of what she believed to be side effects. Once he was old enough to have his own way, he stopped all contact with mental-health professionals and refused all medication.

Although he was impaired socially, he was, for much of his life, not entirely incapable of interacting socially – at least with family members, some teachers and occasional peers. He managed to progress through his primary school education at Sandy Hook, where teachers recognised his social difficulties and attempted to remedy them. They did not, however, consider him grossly abnormal. In secondary school, things became more problematic. He showed an almost complete inability to engage in group activities, either in the classroom or in sport. He became more obviously isolated, leading the school to express concerns to his mother, urging her to accept professional help. At times this led to conflict between the boy and his mother; she responded by withdrawing him from school for periods of homeschooling.

His elder brother progressed through school and continued on to university. The future killer graduated from secondary school, but was recognised as lacking the basic social and educational attainments to follow his brother's example. It is known that he had expressed an ambition to join the military, but not whether he attempted to enlist. He never obtained employment of any kind; after leaving high school, his life was spent largely in his bedroom or visiting a gun club with his mother for target shooting. The only exception was intermittent contact with the one friend he had retained, until a few months before the massacre.

After separation from the family, the boy's father continued contact with both his sons at least until 2010, when the future Sandy

Hook killer decided to break off all further interaction. Interviewed after the tragedy, his father indicated that, although his son had always tended to be somewhat odd and solitary, those behaviours had become much more pronounced in the last couple of years of their relationship. At much the same time, the boy also broke off contact with his older brother. Enquiry revealed that even his interactions with his mother, with whom he lived, had been deteriorating for some time, to the point where, in the months before the attack, email had become their usual means of communication.

Over the years of his schooling, the killer had made occasional friends and acquaintances. One in particular remained in contact with him until a month or so before the shootings. This young man described his friend as shy, with a dry sense of humour. The pair's main shared activity was to visit a local arcade occasionally to play *Dance Dance Revolution*, a game in which players dance to music on a platform, placing their feet on various circles as they light up. (It promotes exercise in the context of shared enjoyment; in Norway, the game is recognised as an official sport.) It is arguably the most benign game in the video firmament.

The same wholesome features do not attach to another of the killer's favourite computer games: *School Shooting*. He played it repeatedly in his bunker of a bedroom. This low-quality product, condemned at the time by most of the gaming community, never established a fan base, and the producers went out of business. Subsequently, better-quality games of a similar ilk have appeared, such as *Destructive Creations*, introduced in 2005. This game revolves around a misanthropic psychopath who plans and carries out a mass killing. Again, the larger gaming community has been highly critical of the product.

The case of the Sandy Hook killer and others indicate that those potentially prone to committing a massacre may latch onto games such as *Destructive Creations*. What is not known is whether they increase the chances that vulnerable individuals will enact the fantasies promoted in the game, or decrease the risks by allowing their harmless discharge. While uncertainty about the potential role of such games remains, I feel we are better off without them.

Like so many lone perpetrators of massacres, the Sandy Hook killer had a long-term fascination with guns, target shooting and, when younger, hunting with his father. His mother shared his interest in guns; as we have noted, they had, in earlier years, regularly gone together to gun clubs. The weapons used in the massacre, and the large number of additional firearms found subsequently at the house, had all been purchased by the mother, using her permit. Evidence obtained from his bedroom established his long-standing fascination with previous school shootings, especially the Columbine massacre.

The last months of his life were spent almost entirely in his bedroom and the adjoining computer room. During this time the windows of both rooms had been taped over with black bin bags. His only communication seems to have been (by email) with his mother. What motivated his final move from fantasy to planning and terrible action, and can only be guessed at from what he left behind. What we do know is that the massacre appears to have been yet another example of a socially isolated, odd gun enthusiast who acted in imitation of previous school massacres, bringing immeasurable grief to the town in which he had grown up, and to the school that had struggled to help him as a child.

*

To date, the university-campus lone mass killing that has produced the greatest loss of life occurred at Virginia Tech, a university in Blacksburg, Virginia. The shooter is, in many ways, a dramatic embodiment of many of the common features of these mass killers.

The atrocity took place on 16 April 2007. It left thirty-two students and faculty staff dead, with a further seventeen injured in the shooting. To the tally of the injured must be added six students who were harmed jumping to safety from their classroom windows on the second floor. Among the murdered were Ryan Clark (twenty-two), Kevin Granata (forty-five) and Matthew Gwaltney (twenty-four). The killer was a twenty-two-year-old student, who committed suicide soon after the police arrived on the scene.

Reports were subsequently produced that provide considerable detail about the events themselves, and about the killer's personal history. Most of the documents, particularly those pertaining to his mental-health records, have not been made public; what is publicly available are the commentaries on materials considered relevant. He left behind a manifesto full of invective, threat and boast. This final testament was in the form of a written document as well as a series of self-recorded videos.

The first clear indication of his interest in school shootings surfaced when he was only fifteen years old. He wrote, in a school essay, about his thoughts of committing both suicide and homicide. In this essay, written shortly after the school massacre at Columbine, he expressed his wish to emulate the Columbine killers. This was the first time – but not the last – that he would put such ideas in writing. The first concrete preparations for launching an attack did not, however, occur until a few months before the killings. Early in 2007 he purchased a Walther semi-automatic pistol. Four weeks later he bought another semi-automatic pistol, this time a Glock. The gap between the first and second gun purchases is to be explained by what Virginia politicians may consider strict gun control laws, which do not allow its citizens to buy potentially people-killing weapons more frequently than once a month. He later purchased large-capacity magazines for both weapons.

On the morning of the massacre, he arose early. He left his dormitory building at about 6.30 AM and walked a short distance to another student residence. There he went up to the fourth floor, and shot and killed two fellow students, Emily Hilscher and Ryan Clark. No connection between the killer and his first two victims has ever been discovered. It is probable that he first shot Hilscher and that, when Clark came to investigate the noise, he was also shot. Hilscher had returned to the dormitory at approximately 7.00 AM, and it is possible that the killer simply followed her up to her room. The shooting occurred about fifteen minutes after she had used her swipe card to enter the building.

As we have seen, it is not unusual for lone-actor massacres to begin with the killing of specific targets before progressing to the murder of additional victims chosen at random. Wagner first killed his wife and children; the University of Texas shooter killed his wife and mother; and the Port Arthur killer targeted an elderly couple against whom he had long harboured a grudge. Perhaps the Virginia Tech murderer had a grudge against Hilscher that others did not know about. He had harassed and stalked a number of female students in the previous three years. Perhaps this young woman was among those who had rejected his unwanted advances. If so, she had not spoken of the incident, even to her long-term boyfriend. (This is not implausible, as some women suffer awkward and inept approaches from insistent males on a regular basis. For them, it becomes part of everyday life. They may also choose not to mention such incidents in part to avoid being regarded as boastful about their own attractiveness.) The most likely explanation, in my opinion, is that this was a victim chosen at random, and for the killer it was in the nature of a practice run for what was to follow.

After killing the two young people, the man left the building without being noticed and returned at 7.17 AM to his own room. He then changed out of his bloodstained clothes. Over the next two hours he worked at his computer, deleting and closing his email account, then deleting the contents of the computer's hard drive before removing and disposing of it. He placed into his backpack the two pistols, some 400 rounds of ammunition in rapid-loading magazines, a hunting knife and several heavy-duty chains.

He then walked to the campus post office, where he sent a package to NBC News containing his written manifesto and a series of videos that he had recorded of himself over the previous weeks. Next, he proceeded to one of the teaching blocks, Norris Hall. He managed to close and chain up the three main entrances to the building from the inside without being observed. He also placed a note on one of the doors, warning that a bomb would go off if anyone tried to remove the chains. The killer then went up to the second floor, where there are several seminar rooms used for teaching small groups of students.

Over the following ten minutes, he murdered twenty-five fellow students and five members of the teaching staff, as well as shooting and injuring a further seventeen students. Several staff members and students were killed or injured while attempting to prevent him from forcing his way into their classrooms. He had fired nearly 200 rounds during this brief, terrifying, chaotic period. As a final act, he shot himself in the head.

The victims were all strangers to him. The classes he targeted were not related to any of the courses he had pursued as a student at the university. None of the faculty members he shot had ever been involved either in teaching him or dealing with him in any other role, anywhere.

Once again, we are faced with the question of what sort of person can, in a carefully planned and executed attack, shoot and kill so many people who have not harmed him in any way – in fact, to whom he was a perfect stranger – at close range, and as they desperately tried to escape.

The future Virginia Tech killer was born in 1984 in South Korea. His parents, together with the eight-year-old boy and his older sister, immigrated to the US in 1992. Even in South Korea, he had been regarded as a quiet, withdrawn child compared with other children – in a culture in which, by Western standards, most children would be considered to be on the quiet side, if not actually subdued. When they arrived in the US, the family had limited facility with English. His sister soon acquired a full command of the language at school, and the parents managed a working knowledge sufficient for their new occupations in a dry-cleaning business. Korean remained the language used at home.

Staff at the school the boy attended became concerned about how little he spoke, either in class or during playtime. His silence was assumed to be attributable to a lack of English fluency; but over time, it became clear that he could, in fact, understand the lessons and prescribed texts, but simply did not speak. He performed well in written tests, but did not contribute verbally in class. Concern grew when he continued to be almost totally isolated among his peers. Even at home, he spoke very little to his parents, and communicated regularly only with his sister.

At the age of twelve he was referred, for the first time, for assessment at a counselling service. Despite many attempts to assist him, and to work with the family, the boy remained painfully shy, isolated and largely mute. When he submitted an essay expressing admiration for the perpetrators of the Columbine massacre, he was referred by the school for a psychiatric evaluation. He was seen by an experienced child psychiatrist who diagnosed a depressive illness with marked anxiety features. He was prescribed antidepressants and entered into ongoing counselling. This counselling, because of his reluctance to speak, was carried out in the form of art therapy.

The medication, combined with the sensible approach to psychotherapy, seems to have produced some improvement. He now managed to speak at school at least in response to direct questions, though he always did so in whispered tones. There was less improvement when it came to socialising with peers; he still appeared to be a painfully anxious and withdrawn adolescent. His school grades were consistently in the top 20 per cent for everything that was not marked on either class participation or verbal interaction. He never established any friendships during his whole school career, and he avoided participating in sporting or other group activities.

He graduated from secondary school with grades sufficient to obtain university entrance, and chose to enrol at Virginia Tech despite being advised that such a large campus, a long way from his parents, might not be the wisest choice. At the beginning of the university year he moved into one of the halls of residence. He would now be living among some 30,000 fellow students. For many young people who have struggled to fit in with their peer group at school, going to university can offer a new start, where at least some of the people around them are likely to share their interests and possess similar abilities and attitudes. No such renaissance occurred for the future killer. He remained isolated, uncommunicative, an alien in an alien land.

He enrolled initially to study information technology, a choice that reflected his strengths during his school years. The following year, despite obtaining reasonable grades in the maths and science units he had taken, he switched to pursuing a major in English Literature. This, one might have thought, based on his previous performance at school, played more to his likely areas of academic weakness rather than strength. The reason he gave the university for the change was that he had developed an interest in poetry, and was intending to write a novel.

Novelists are not always the most talkative and sociable people, with some preserving their communication largely for their writing. The young man's decision, therefore, was not necessarily foolish. The difficulty that pursuing such a course entailed was that, in classes in literature and particularly in the unit he took in creative writing, great emphasis was placed on oral presentation and class discussion. He had the requisite enthusiasm for literature, but his grades at the end of the year were poor, particularly when compared with those he had previously received in the maths- and science-based subjects. He did, in fact, soon after, submit a proposal for a novel to a New York publisher. Nothing was to come from this initiative.

He lived in the university's dormitory accommodation but had little contact even with students with whom he shared a suite. He simply did not respond to their attempts to engage him, and declined to eat in their company. In classes, he was also unresponsive both to fellow students and to teachers. At one point in his second year he took to wearing reflective sunglasses in class, with a hat pulled down to further obscure his face. One of the teachers insisted that he stop coming to class dressed in this disconcerting manner, because it was disturbing to his fellow students. He responded to this request by arriving on the following occasion with a scarf wrapped around his head and face in the manner of a Bedouin. He avoided speaking in class whenever possible. When he had no choice but to read his work aloud, he did so in the almost inaudible whisper that he had perfected during his school years.

It was not only his unusual manner of dress that caused concern – after all, eccentricities of dress are, for some, part of being a student. The real worry concerned the nature of some of the written assignments he had submitted. One, for example, consisted of an angry rant directed at classmates, whom he called "low-life barbarians" who disgusted him and whom he labelled "despicable disgraces to the human race". He also wrote that he hoped his fellow students "would burn in hell". This being a university, a number of committee meetings were convened to discuss the offensive essays and other problems centred around this troubling student. These deliberations were followed by approaches to both encourage the young man to submit less offensive essays and to urge him to seek help from the student health services.

He caused anxiety on campus as well as in class. He had stalked a number of female students, in a manner typical of the incompetent suitor. He repeatedly followed, approached and attempted to communicate with women he found attractive, usually by email or notes, persisting even when it was made clear that his attentions were unwanted. He continued in at least one case even after the woman made it very plain that she found him frightening. He stopped the behaviour, however, either when he was challenged by someone in authority or when enough time had passed even for him to recognise the futility of the pursuit.

Despite his stalking behaviours, none of the victims pursued criminal charges against the man, although several asked campus police to speak to him. One of his victims did report the harassment to her father, who contacted campus police with his concerns. Thus, in early December 2005, the police called on him in his room and warned him of the consequences should he continue. Following this visit from the police, he texted one of his roommates that he might kill himself. This student quite properly informed the university of this potential suicide threat. The report triggered another visit from the police, who took the future killer to be assessed at a local mental-health facility.

He was then sectioned for a period under Virginia's mental-health act to allow for assessment and consideration of further treatment – either as a voluntary patient or, if deemed necessary, on a compulsory basis. A psychiatrist and a psychologist both considered that he had a mood disorder, though they seem to have differed on whether or not this was of a type that would constitute mental illness within the meaning of Virginia's mental-health legislation. They did not, however, consider that he was a threat either to himself or others, so he could not be detained or treated without his consent. The psychiatrist recorded in his notes that he had found no evidence for the presence of any psychotic features such as delusions or hallucinations.

Without seeing the medical records, it is impossible even to guess at exactly what was found, or how thorough the enquiry was, or even how frank the young man was in his answers to the various questions. He was discharged from hospital on 14 December without any medication having been prescribed, but he was referred for a course of psychotherapy. No such psychotherapy ever occurred.

He returned to Virginia Tech for the 2006 spring semester. His behaviour remained much the same, and the content of some of his written assignments continued to be troubling. In one composition, his main character discusses using semi-automatics and machine guns to "kill every goddamn person in this goddamn school". As the assignment was intended to be a work of fiction, this and other parts of the text did not amount to a threat to kill – at least in law. Understandably, however, it and other similar pieces of writing caused disquiet among his teachers. The teachers did what they could, which was to urge him to seek help and counsel him about the inappropriate nature of some of his written submissions.

Over the next two semesters, he remained isolated from other students, ignoring all attempts to persuade him to seek counselling;

he stalked women occasionally for a brief period as well, though most of these episodes were only brought to the attention of Virginia Tech officials after the massacre. University staff members continued to try and persuade him to seek counselling, and he continued to ignore all such suggestions.

What is known about him at this point is largely what he was *not*. He was unable to socialise even at a basic level; to bring himself to seek counselling or help from mental-health services; or to establish any kind of romantic connection. He was not succeeding academically, at least not at a level that reflected his apparent intellectual abilities. He was not thought to be psychotic, though he was considered to have a mood disorder. Above all, what is most unclear is why this man was so interpersonally disabled.

Perhaps insights into his internal world had been glimpsed through his more disconcerting writings; reports prepared in retrospect highlight communications that seem to indicate violent propensities, and which contain rage-filled utterances. There must have also been many examples of more mundane written submissions, with at least a modicum of academic merit – else he would not have obtained reasonable grades in some of his English courses. Without access to the full range of his written work at the university, it is impossible to know whether the troubled and troubling pieces were occasional aberrations or a significant proportion of his output.

Inevitably, what colours our view of him as he prepared to commit a massacre are the written and video-recorded testaments he left behind. Only extracts from the text of his manifesto sent to NBC News are available on public websites. Similarly, only extracts from the videos can be accessed. Some experts have concluded that the manifesto indicates that he was in a psychotic state when he committed the massacre. That was also my immediate response when, soon after the event, I read parts of the manifesto and viewed the videos that were released. On returning to these materials with the additional benefit of information that has been published subsequently, I am far less sure about the nature of his state of mind on that terrible day.

A number of commentators consider that parts of the manifesto indicate that he suffered from delusions of grandeur. It is true that he compares himself to Moses and Jesus Christ. An important point, however, is that his claim to be like Moses is because he will become a leader, and the comparison to Jesus is because he, too, had endured great suffering and will inspire future generations. He does not claim to *be* a Moses, or a Christ figure, or even to have any unique connection to these embodiments of the divine. These claims are certainly ostentatious, but there is no evidence that he believed himself to be endowed with special powers; typically, in cases of religious grandiose delusions, such a claim is actually present. He does not claim to have private access to the Almighty's intentions and desires.

Considering his bombastic claims in context, I think a case can be made for their being metaphorical. After all, he studied poetry and aspired to becoming a writer. One clear aspect of the published parts of the manifesto is that the language he uses echoes that of the Bible. The only book found in his room after the massacre was a New Testament. He wrote that he would die like Jesus Christ, but made no claims about resurrection. He described his enemies as the "Apostles of Sin" and informed us he would join fellow martyrs, naming the Columbine killers.

The manifesto and the videos seem to me to constitute the kind of rant typical of a figure defined by novelist and academic Michael André Bernstein as the "abject hero". The killer wrote that "his" people were the weak, the defenceless and the innocent. He believed that he would inspire such individuals to become an "avenging Phoenix". He said: "We will sacrifice our lives to fuck you thousandfold for what you have done to us." It is in the nature of abject heroes, in finally asserting themselves, to claim both the crown of leadership and the halo of martyrdom. It is also typical to shift the responsibility for their acts of violence onto others. The killer expressed this directly when he wrote: "What did you expect me to do, you violators of human rights?" The pent-up rage at others, but above all at himself for not retaliating, exploded on that April morning in a massacre.

In retrospect, it is all too easy to construct warning signs out of his previous words and actions. Yet most were neither missed nor ignored – he was recognised even as a child to be troubled and withdrawn, and at a very early stage he was described as suffering from severe social anxiety. It is not difficult to imagine a vicious circle developing: the more he would have withdrawn in fear from those around him, the more he would have drawn attention to himself, which in turn would made him withdraw further. This response would have occurred irrespective of whether the attentions he attracted were motivated by the wish to help or the wish to torment.

In the reports prepared afterwards there is considerable breast-beating about the failures to intervene earlier, though it is usually other people's breasts that receive the beating. Behind the *mea culpas* and the blaming are often unrealistic sets of expectations about what could have been achieved by any conceivable intervention. There is, of course, the entirely understandable drive to discover factors that might be used in the future to identify and manage those who are at risk of behaving homicidally. I fully share such aspirations, but suspect that, in these reports – as in so many similar postmortems – the committees were looking in the wrong places.

A number of other lone-actor mass killers have been recognised in early childhood as having problems relating both with adults and other children. In the case of the Virginia Tech killer, several attempts were made to assist, which were largely ineffective. As an adolescent, he was deemed to have significant emotional problems, and again appropriate actions were undertaken that helped to some extent – at least in the short term. He received sensible advice about the best choice of university and courses. He chose to ignore them, as was his right. At university, his problems were noted, and he was urged to seek counselling and think again about the appropriateness of the courses he had chosen to take. Again, he ignored this advice. The university could have excluded him on the basis of his behaviour both in class and around campus. They generously chose to try to help rather than reject him.

One of the few points at which it would have been possible to compel him to do what others discerned to be in his best interests was in December 2005, when he was committed to a psychiatric hospital. I do not know how much the mental-health professionals who assessed him knew about his troubling writings or his stalking behaviours. I do not know if he admitted to any murderous fantasies. Even if those assessing him had been told, though, what could they have done? For him to have been detained under the mental-health act, the psychiatrist would have had to give evidence to a court that decides such matters in Virginia that the man was both mentally ill and dangerous to himself or others. Even if this had happened, and the court had accepted that opinion, in practice the killer would have been unlikely to have been detained for more than a few days.

The only hope at this stage for an effective intervention would have been persuading him to enter long-term outpatient treatment. It is possible to compel such ongoing therapeutic engagements, though it is far more difficult than when the patient voluntarily seeks help. In reality, there was nothing that could have been done without using the powers of the mental health act to force his cooperation as the first stage to establishing a longer-term therapeutic relationship.

One thing that should have happened as a result of his detention under the mental-health act was that he be prohibited from buying or possessing guns of the type used in the massacre. Had the legally required checks been performed properly when he attempted to obtain his weapons, he would not have been allowed to complete the purchase. He could have gone to a local gun show and still bought these weapons legally, or he could have travelled across state lines to acquire the weapons. The law did not function as it was designed to function, but then the laws, like those of so many US states, are no great barrier to people obtaining guns designed to kill other people, even if they do have an official history of having been committed to hospitals because of mental illness. This situation is made worse because some experts overlook the overwhelming evidence of an association between psychotic illness and violence, including homicidal violence, and continue to advise governments on the basis of their fallacious beliefs. This is an example of one group's good intentions paving the way to someone else's hell.

CHAPTER 8

Massacres in the workplace

ONE OF THE first workplace massacres took place in Miami, Florida in August 1982. A disgruntled customer opened fire with a pump-action shotgun in a welding shop, killing eight workers and injuring three others before being killed by police. Informants suggested he had had a long-standing grudge against the workshop for having overcharged him $20 for repairs on his lawnmower.

This massacre was followed by a series of workplace shootings in which the most common factor was rage, engendered by conflict with management or coworkers. In August 1983, a man opened fire at a South Carolina post office where he was employed, killing and wounding fellow workers. Post office workers launched other murderous attacks at their workplaces in December 1983 in Alabama, March 1984 in Atlanta and August 1986 in Oklahoma.

In the years 1983–87, twelve workplace massacres involved US Postal Service (USPS) employees or ex-employees. That is over 50 per cent of workplace massacres, and over 20 per cent of all active shooter events in those years. The phrase *going postal* was, for a while, applied to all lone-actor attacks in the workplace as a result.

A significant proportion of basic-grade jobs in the USPS had traditionally been occupied by ex-servicemen. Various explanations for this have been proposed, from the wish to remain in uniform to the more convincing suggestion of a desire to continue in government employment providing job security and cast-iron pension entitlements. The fact that many veterans were already working for the Post Office may also have encouraged those leaving the armed forces to apply. It may, furthermore, have increased their chances of being hired. (The influence of personal contacts in obtaining blue-collar jobs is usually even more marked than in managerial and professional appointments.) In many areas of the postal service, this resulted in a shop-floor culture reflecting both the virtues and the problems of male veterans.

In the 1980s and 1990s, the USPS went through massive restructuring, which brought not just redundancies but also increasing managerial encroachment on the autonomy that had been part of the work environment. The job security and pension entitlements that had compensated up till then for the relatively low pay were also beginning to be eroded. Larger numbers of women, particularly in managerial roles, may have brought added tension to the existing male-dominated workforce. Tens of thousands of men were adversely affected by the USPS restructuring. Many were probably enraged by these changes. Twelve individuals are recorded as having responded over these years by perpetrating a lone-actor massacre – an extremely low proportion of the workforce, but a remarkably large proportion of all workplace mass shootings during this period. Of these events involving postal workers, 60 per cent ended in the suicide of the shooter.

Expose enough people to loss of job security, loss of status and the removal of the supports on which they have built their hopes for retirement, and most will become angry; some will become depressed or suicidal; and occasionally, one or more may also become homicidal. If the culture has developed a script for murder-suicide in response to such rage and resentment, every so often that script will be adopted. The script in the post office shootings, and in most other workplace massacres, is not exactly the same as that which lies behind some other lone-actor massacres. Those who target strangers in public spaces tend to be driven by the desire for fame (albeit posthumous fame), and are expressing a rejection of society as a whole. Workplace massacres are not about grandiose fantasies of dying in a hail of bullets, or about the power and destructiveness of the shooter: they seem to be more about restoring lost prestige in the eyes of coworkers.

The motive is often connected to wreaking revenge on a particular organisation and its functionaries. It is a *fuck the lot of you and exit stage left* performance. The postal workers, like the perpetrators of most workplace massacres, were playing primarily to a small audience of coworkers, managers and acquaintances. They were not usually performing "both for the thousands in attendance and the millions watching around the world", to borrow a phrase from Michael Buffer, a prominent American boxing announcer. However, without the script encompassing a larger picture inaugurated by the likes of the University of Texas gunman, this more modest model of murder-suicide may well never have emerged in our societies.

There are three types of workplace massacre: the first occurs at an establishment where the killer is employed or has previously been employed; in the second, the killer goes to the workplace of their partner or ex-partner; and the third takes place on the premises of an organisation where the murderer was never employed, but against which they have a grievance.

The most common motive involves a grudge against the employer, an employee or coworkers. In some cases, the massacre is the culmination of a long campaign of complaint and litigation in which the perpetrators are abnormally persistent complainants or, to use our psychiatric term, querulants (from the Latin *querulus*, "complaining", "mumbling").

*

One of the most dramatic mass killers of the querulant type was a Swiss man who, on 28 September 2001, entered the regional parliament building in the canton of Zug, where he shot and killed fourteen people and injured sixteen more. The victims included Dorly Heimgartner (fifty-four), Jean-Paul Flachsmann (sixty-five) and Käthi Langenegger (fifty-nine).

The Zug killer had gained entry dressed as a policeman and was armed with an assault rifle, with which he sprayed bullets into the council chamber where the local government was in session. Depending on which account you accept, the episode ended either when he detonated a homemade bomb, killing himself and injuring several more bystanders, or immediately after the explosion when he shot himself.

The killer had been in dispute with the local authority for several years over an occurrence involving one of its employees. The nature of the original incident has been described in somewhat different terms by various sources. All agree there was an argument: some say on a bus with the driver, some in a bar with an employee of the transport agency, some that it wasn't a bus driver but a government chauffeur. The disagreement may have been over the man not paying his fare, or accusing the bus driver of being drunk. Some sources say he pulled a gun, some that there was only a heated exchange. In cases involving querulants, it is not unusual for the details of the initial grievance to be lost among later elaborations of the supposed injustice or injury.

What everyone seems to agree on is that the man subsequently made complaint after complaint, and attempted to litigate against the government transport department. These complaints generated vast piles of paperwork and consumed an immense amount of time for those attempting to resolve them. The grievance escalated over the years from the man having been mistreated to being deliberately victimised, and finally to being the object of organised persecution by the government. The redress he sought grew from an official apology to the dismissal of the driver to the removal of the CEO and minister responsible for the transport authority and, finally, to the addition of compensation payment with the amount demanded increasing month by month. In short, it was the typical progression of a querulant's pursuit of their notion of justice and personal vindication. Equally typical was the total disruption of this man's own life as he subordinated everything to his quest.

At the time of the massacre, the killer was fifty-seven years old – which, though old for a mass shooter, is commonplace enough as an age for querulants to come to notice, which most frequently happens following some act of civil disobedience to publicise their case. This, in turn, leads to their arrest and prosecution. He had worked previously as a salesman. He had been convicted of various offences in his twenties, including theft and sexual offences, for which he had received a total of eighteen months in prison. There were no subsequent convictions. He had been married with one child, but the couple separated either just before he began his campaign of complaining, or not long after. He had been involved in a previous campaign for justice, but this one was on behalf of a neighbour who, if the reports are correct, had very good grounds to seek redress from the government. (In some reports in the Swiss press, he was referred to as a criminal psychopath, for what that is worth.)

Querulant complainers often reach a point at which they decide the only way to progress their quest for justice is to resort to illegal action aimed at dramatising their plight. These are almost always acts of criminal damage, trespass, threat issuance or, occasionally, assault. If they resort to killing, it is usually a matter of killing themselves: in one of the cases I was involved with, the querulant shot himself in front of a public official he blamed for obstructing the resolution of his complaints. What, then, were the factors that pushed the Zug killer in the direction of mass murder?

It has been suggested that the terrorist attacks in the US on 11 September 2001 may have encouraged him to resort to violence. This seems unlikely. More relevant is that he had developed a fascination with guns. He had acquired his first gun licence in 1996, though there is a suggestion that he had previously obtained weapons illegally. He ended up with a veritable arsenal that included semi-automatics, pistols and a pump-action shotgun.

It can be difficult to tell, in the abnormally persistent complainant, where the boundary lies between the self-righteous, obsessive pursuit of a grievance and the delusional belief that you are involved in a death-or-glory struggle for justice against organised persecution – not only for yourself but on behalf of the whole community. The Zug killer may have progressed into the realms of delusion; certainly the manifesto he left behind to explain his actions suggests he had gone well beyond the limits of reason and reality. He had become increasingly socially isolated and impoverished over the years of pursuing his campaign against the canton government. Angry, aggrieved, socially isolated, desperate, deluded and gun-obsessed – that will do it.

*

As noted above, there are also cases that involve a stalker entering the workplace of their ex-partner or desired lover, first killing them and then proceeding to shoot coworkers and sometimes passers-by in the vicinity. The most common category of stalker to indulge in such intrusions is the rejected type, who pursues an ex-partner out of a mixture of motives related both to anger and to the desire for reconciliation. Some launch attacks not only on the ex-partner but on coworkers who try to prevent them gaining access to their target.

The best-documented case of a workplace massacre in the context of stalking did not involve a rejected type, but another type that may be termed the *intimacy-seeking stalker*. In 1988 a computer technician at a large Sunnyvale, California factory, shot and killed seven coworkers and wounded four. Among the victims were Wayne "Buddy" Williams, Jr (twenty-three), Helen Lamparter (forty-nine) and Ronald G. Doney (thirty-six). The killer had become infatuated with a coworker, Ms A, who was the first to be shot – though luckily she survived her injuries. He had made repeated attempts to start a relationship with Ms A. Despite clear refusals and numerous requests for him to stop pestering her, he had continued to approach her, write to her, phone her and intrude on her repeatedly – for nearly four years.

The Sunnyvale killer was a shy, socially incompetent man who, in adult life, had never managed to establish an intimate relationship or even any lasting friendships. He seems to have abandoned the search for any real type of relationship, substituting an all-encompassing fantasy that his love for Ms A would, despite so many indications to the contrary, eventually be realised when she finally returned his affections. Disaster followed his ultimate recognition that these dreams would never come to pass. He was said to be a rigid individual with a long-standing fascination with guns. In the months before the shooting, he had become increasingly threatening towards Ms A, and was awaiting trial on charges related to this behaviour.

That over 20 per cent of lone-actor workplace massacres may be related to either stalking or querulous complaining suggests a role for mental health. The first point to note is that stalkers and querulants reveal themselves both by their behaviour and their utterances. In both, there is usually an extended period in which they pursue their quest, be it for vindication or affection, in an obsessive manner not only obvious to those they are pursuing, but inevitably involving actual or potential breaches of criminal law. They harass, stalk and issue direct or thinly veiled threats. This behaviour offers a chance to recognise the risk, and in most cases opens up the possibility of using the law to ensure that appropriate mental-health assessments and treatment are undertaken.

The sad fact is that stalking, particularly by rejected ex-partners, is still not always accorded the concern it merits. Victims often delay too long before reporting stalkers to the police, or even telling family and friends about the unwanted and distressing intrusions. The police and courts make less-than-optimal use of forensic mental-health expertise in assessing and managing the risk presented by stalkers. This reflects, in part, a paucity of suitably trained professionals willing to undertake this work. The same problems, but to an even more marked extent, impair the effective response to querulants, even when they have progressed to active harassment and threats. The number of mental-health professionals willing and able to assess and manage querulants is even smaller than those who will accept referrals of stalkers.

Improving forensic mental-health services' ability to manage both stalkers and querulants, and the courts' use of such expertise, would advance our ability to protect the victims as well as help free their pursuers from the obsessive behaviour that ruins their lives. Though such advances might make only a small contribution to reducing lone-actor mass killings, it would make a significant one to managing the thousands caught up in the distress and dangers attendant in stalking and querulous complaining.

Examining the available information on the lone-actor workplace massacres motivated by grudges against an employer or coworkers suggests certain other commonalities beyond the place in which the massacre occurred. In the run-up to the murders, the perpetrators are often found to have talked to friends and acquaintances about shooting particular individuals at their workplace. Some have uttered direct threats in the days and weeks before the killings.

Talk of committing a workplace massacre has almost always been regarded at the time as just that: talk. In part, this reflects the norms of males socialising in groups in which it is not particularly unusual to speak casually of wanting to kill those who are currently causing the speaker grief (*I could kill the bastards*). However, the tolerance of such behaviour, with the assumption of its being of no consequence, has changed dramatically with the increasing awareness of the very events we have discussed.

CHAPTER 9

Terrorists

IT SEEMS ALMOST inevitable that lone mass killers would emerge who claimed they were acting on behalf of specific terrorist or extremist groups. Lone-actor terrorists are a hybrid of those who *are* members of terrorist groups, and those who commit massacres without claiming any ideological justification. Terrorists, with a few notable exceptions, have until recently been socially integrated into organisations with shared ideas and aims. In recent years, however, we have seen a rapid increase in attacks by lone terrorists, who, as the name implies, are not members of organisations and do not have direct personal or social links to other members of a terrorist network. Their radicalisation has not occurred through the medium of inclusion into a group of like-minded enthusiasts, but usually via the solitary study of radical postings on the internet and in literature.

In 2009, a US Army psychiatrist shot forty-five fellow servicemen at Fort Hood, Texas, killing thirteen, including Captain John P. Gaffaney (fifty-six), Michael G. Cahill (sixty-two) and Jason D. Hunt (twenty-two). The massacre was brought to an end when the killer himself was shot. He survived his injuries and, at trial, though he offered no defence, he stated he had acted in support of *jihad* against the enemy of Islam. He was, on the face of it, very different from others who commit lone-actor massacres. He was a doctor in the Army

Medical Corps in his late thirties who had recently been promoted to the rank of major. Despite spending almost all his adult life in the Army, he had never shown any interest in guns and had avoided the shooting ranges.

He was born in the US, his parents having emigrated from Palestine. There is little information available about his home life, but he is reported to have been isolated at school. He joined the United States Cadet Corps in his teens and, after finishing a science degree, joined the Army full-time. His medical education and subsequent psychiatric training were sponsored by the Army. He never married, and does not appear to have made close friends or even to have socialised much with either his military or medical colleagues. At Fort Hood, he chose to live in rather basic accommodation away from the base, rather than the far more salubrious housing he was entitled to use on the base.

He was a practising Muslim, and his level of religious observance seems to have increased markedly in the months before the massacre. During his time at Fort Hood, he is said to have attended a local mosque on an almost daily basis. He was not, however, involved in social and religious groups associated with the mosque, remaining aloof from his fellow worshippers. Middle-aged, professional men in stable employment who attend religious services do not fit the usual profile of a mass killer, even if they are not particularly sociable.

There is another perspective on the Fort Hood killer. He qualified in medicine and obtained his board certification in psychiatry, but only with difficulty. At medical school he was consistently in the bottom 25 per cent of students. His progress after qualification can only be described as slow. He managed poorly as a psychiatric resident and received several warnings about his inadequate performance. There are reports that fellow students and residents described him variously as aloof, disconnected, belligerent and schizoid. These traits might not have been a great disadvantage in some areas of medical practice, but were likely to be problematic in psychiatry. There are also reports that he had repeatedly complained of abuse for being a Muslim. He claimed on occasion to have been the victim of what amounted to an orchestrated campaign of racial and religious prejudice, as he may well have been.

Some three years before the killing, he began sending emails to a well-known radical Islamic cleric, the New Mexico-born Anwar al-Awlaki (who was later killed in Yemen in a US drone attack). The Fort Hood psychiatrist's various communications to al-Awlaki are far from clear in terms of what he was asking or his own views on the teachings of this jihadist figure. In any event, he received no replies to his missives.

The killer had also viewed a number of what might be termed radical Islamic websites. The Army knew about his interest in Islamic terrorist groups and extremist preachers. He had claimed to be accessing such material to learn more about potential threats to the US. At one point it seems that the Army considered grooming him for a role in counterterrorism. Blogs and writings by the likes of al-Awlaki may simply have provided a narrative that allowed a resentful, despairing man to reframe his predicament as part of the worldwide persecution of the Faithful, and to translate being trapped in a hopeless impasse into an escape into martyrdom.

The likely precipitant of the attack came when the psychiatrist received a posting to Afghanistan. He had made requests *not* to be transferred there, and so appealed against it, citing religious and political objections. He even explored the possibility of being granted an honourable discharge from the Army to avoid it. Both his appeal and his request for a discharge were denied, and he was ordered to prepare himself for transfer shortly before the massacre.

Terrorist or lone mass killer? Obviously both – but which are the critical elements in the making of this particular tragedy? Some of the relevant factors are unrelated to terrorism. He was an isolated, difficult man who felt rejected, if not actively persecuted, by those among whom he lived and worked. Despite appearances, he was in many ways a professional failure. He cannot have been unaware how easily his status as an officer and a doctor could slip away. He almost certainly realised that if he refused the posting to Afghanistan, he could face the possibility of a dishonourable discharge, and thus considerable difficulties in establishing a career in either private or public medical practice. He found himself trapped in a situation in which he had to choose between compromising his beliefs and risking the end of his professional and military career.

Also important on his road to becoming a mass killer was not so much his Islamic faith but his flirtation with jihadist and ultra-radical ideas. As with so many lone mass killers, this was a socially isolated man who believed he had to live with rejection and failure because of the antagonism of others. He may have become a religious enthusiast, then tempted by martyrdom. Trapped by his posting to Afghanistan in what was for him an intolerable dilemma, he chose to escape by adopting a terrorist variant of the lone-mass-killer script.

Adam Yahiye Gadahn, an American convert to Islam and an al-Qaeda spokesman, described the Fort Hood killer as "a pioneer, trailblazer, and a role model for every Muslim who finds himself among unbelievers". This socially awkward, marginally competent doctor, who had chosen to spend nearly twenty years serving in the US military, was reconstructed by Gadahn as a martyr in the struggle against the very organisation that had nurtured his career and supported him to that point. The psychiatrist came to believe that in some way the world in general, and the Army in particular, had failed to recognise and sufficiently reward his abilities: that the Army paid his way through both medical school and postgraduate training, later promoting him to the rank of major, was not enough. Such gifts could be understood as grounds for gratitude and loyalty, but not for him. What we know of this man's history suggests he was, from adolescence, consumed by resentment.

Even in cases where violence might be considered legitimate, it is balanced against the reluctance to harm oneself and others. Usually, the factors tipping the balance are social and psychological as much as intellectual conviction – all the more so in lone mass killers, who are not drawn by close personal relationships and shared commitments into joining their comrades in deadly combat. The Fort Hood killer is a role model for the resentful, despairing failures of the world who fool themselves that they can convert their suicide into some form of personal vindication. He *is* a martyr – but only to his own grandiosity and paranoia, not to any religious or political cause.

*

Separating the contribution of psychopathologies and social pathologies from ideological commitments in one case, that of a married couple who committed a massacre in San Bernardino, California, in December 2015, is even more difficult than the case of the Army psychiatrist. In the immediate aftermath of the San Bernardino shooting, a commentator on CNN expressed the fear that we were seeing the emergence of a crossover between workplace massacre and terrorist attack. Workplace massacres, or any other lone-perpetrator massacre, had not previously been perpetrated by married couples who were university graduates, financially secure and had recently become parents for the first time. The picture that emerged over the months since this massacre is one of the intertwining of religious fanaticism and some of the types of personal vulnerability found so often among lone shooters.

The husband, Y, was born in the US of immigrant parents from Pakistan. He had a troubled and disrupted home environment marred by domestic violence, which had eventually led to his parents separating. He is described as having been a lonely child, ostracised and sometimes actively bullied by his school fellows. He is only known to have had one real friend, M, a young man of seventeen at the time to Y's twenty-four, whom he met through a mutual interest in cars and car maintenance. M later related that he fell under Y's influence to such an extent that he even converted to Islam so they could attend mosque together.

M claims that as early as 2011, Y, the future killer, had spoken about his desire to become a martyr for God. He was, apparently, looking at radical Islamic websites and expressing his admiration for jihadist groups such as al-Qaeda. He seems to have shared considerable details with his friend about his death-and-glory fantasies. M, by his own account, was himself drawn into making plans with Y for a terrorist outrage, proceeding as far as the acquisition of suitable weapons for such an attack. At the same time, some local men were arrested in connection with possible terrorist activities. Neither Y nor M had any links to these men, but M was sufficiently scared by the events for him to – in his own words – "come to [his] senses". He subsequently broke off all contact with his onetime co-conspirator.

Perhaps partly in reaction to the loss of his only friend, Y began, at this time, to search for a suitable Muslim bride using the relevant internet sites. Through one of these sites he made contact with Z, his future wife. They communicated for a while by email and then, in 2013, he travelled to Saudi Arabia both to meet her and to make his Hajj pilgrimage. Subsequently they married, and Z came to the US on a marriage visa about eighteen months before the shootings.

Y had obtained a degree in Environmental Health, and later worked for the San Bernardino Health Department as an inspector – a modest job with a modest salary. He had been in this position for eight years at the time of the shooting. There were known to have been some tensions with work colleagues; these were sometimes provoked by Y's advocacy of unpopular views about US policy in the Middle East, and sometimes by forcefully expressed opinions to the contrary from some coworkers.

Y had never been a hunter, but had a long-term passion for guns, which he collected and used in local shooting ranges. As far back as 2011, if M is to be believed, Y was toying with the idea of making bombs: when the police raided his home after the massacre, a number of homemade explosive devices were discovered.

Y worshiped regularly at a local mosque, where he does not seem to have developed much in the way of contact with his co-religionists; his move, early in 2015, to a much smaller mosque may have been related to objections made to the extremist and jihadist ideas he had been expressing at his regular place of worship. There is little doubt that, over many years, Y had articulated his support for jihadist terrorism. He was found after the massacre to have accessed a variety of extremist websites, and in particular Anwar al-Awlaki's blogs. Despite what he said about his radical political views, there is no evidence that he ever made direct contact with any member of an extremist Islamic group, let alone a terrorist organisation. He did not even go as far as the Fort Hood killer in attempting email contact with advocates of jihad.

We know even less about Z. She was born in Pakistan but grew up in Saudi Arabia, where her father was employed as an engineer. She attended a girls' school in Saudi Arabia that catered for the families of the well-to-do, providing an education that emphasised fundamentalist Islamic views and strict adherence to the Qur'an. (The school has denied that she ever attended, and the Saudi government denied that she ever lived in the country.) She went to university in Pakistan, where she obtained a Pharmacy degree. (These facts are not disputed by either the university or the Pakistani government.) She does not seem to have worked at any time as a pharmacist, however.

Z is believed to have visited extremist, jihadist websites while in Saudi Arabia, despite Saudi assertions to the contrary. It is uncertain whether or not she had had any direct contact with these groups. She continued to access radical websites after her move to the US. She made no effort to integrate into American society – quite the contrary. She isolated herself almost completely, rarely leaving the marital home except to travel by car with her husband to the mosque. She is described as having dressed completely covered, including her face, and often remained in the car while her husband was at prayer. There is a report that she accompanied her husband to the shooting range, as well.

There is good evidence that Y and Z had planned and prepared for some time to commit a terrorist act. The health department's Christmas party, where the attack ultimately took place, may or may not have been their chosen target. Certainly, the accumulation of bombs as well as guns suggests a more wide-ranging, complex operation. It is reported that on the day of the event, Y went to the Christmas party. At some point, not long after his arrival, a heated argument broke out with a coworker about Middle East politics. Y then left the party, only to return an hour or so later with Z. By this time they were both dressed in combat garb, and armed with semi-automatic rifles. Upon entering, they immediately began shooting into the crowd of partygoers, killing fourteen and injuring twenty-two. Among the victims were Juan Espinoza (fifty), Bennetta Betbadal (forty-six) and Sierra Clayborn (twenty-seven).

After discharging their weapons, the couple attempted to escape in their car; they drove around randomly until their eventual confrontation with local police, in which they were killed.

There had been no recent crisis to bring the pair to resort to violence. Both had entertained notions of committing terrorism for a number of years. There is some evidence that Y, at least, had fantasised about becoming a religious martyr. He was an angry, damaged man, resentful and convinced he was being disadvantaged, if not actively persecuted, for his religion and ethnicity. We know little about Z as a person: she was an immigrant in a country whose customs and culture she rejected. She had no social life and no immediate family other than her husband's. She was physically in the US, but for those eighteen months she did not in any sense 'live' there. The stresses of immigration are considerable for anyone, but for this woman they must have been particularly severe.

On hearing that the killers had left behind their baby, my wife's first reaction – and that of many people, I suspect – was, "How could they do such a thing?" By that she did not just mean abandoning their child, but also deliberately killing other people's children and other children's parents. (I have found that women hold women to higher standards than men, which sadly reflects the reality of male versus female behaviour.) One could speculate that having a child might have brought hope and joy into their isolated, beleaguered existence. On the other hand, rather than relieving their distress, alienation and anger, perhaps it amplified those feelings in these two disturbed people. I have no basis for these speculations; it is a struggle to understand what remains largely unanswered.

*

The definition of terrorism favoured by the FBI is "the unlawful use of force or violence against persons or property to intimidate or coerce a government, the civilian population, or any segment thereof, in furtherance of political or social objectives". This definition has the great advantages of clarity and brevity. The difficulty lies not in its ability to encompass everything we would wish to label "terrorist", but in its potential to capture a wide range of other political activities that only dictatorships and authoritarian governments would wish to criminalise.

As a schoolboy, I sat down in the street at Trafalgar Square in London with the philosopher Bertrand Russell. Admittedly, this was not exactly up close and personal with my hero – I was there together with hundreds of others to protest against the proliferation of nuclear weapons. We were sitting in the road to disrupt traffic in central London. Our passive resistance became remarkably active when the police attempted to remove us. The intention was to cause chaos and gain wide publicity in order to pressure the British government into giving up nuclear weapons. Later, the Campaign for Nuclear Disarmament became even more militant, and involved some of us in actions such as physical confrontation with the police, property damage and the distribution of a stolen report – classified as "top secret" – on the government's plans in the event of a nuclear attack. (This report was of such callous absurdity that even a satirist as cruel as Jonathan Swift would have blushed to pen such a work.)

The press condemned and insulted us, and some waxed on about contempt for the law. However, they never resorted to the word *terrorist*. Yet demonstrations and actions similar in character, if not in purpose, are now regularly called "terrorist" in oppressive regimes such as Turkey and Russia, to say nothing of those on the streets of

London, Melbourne and Washington, DC – and, arguably, they do fall within the FBI definition.

The wide scope of definitions of terrorism not only encourages governments and the media to strip legitimacy from political protest, but also leads to a wide range of political activity acquiring this label. One interesting sub-group that pops up on some terrorist databases is that of protesting farmers. Dwight Watson, who appeared on some terrorist lists, was a US tobacco farmer who in 2003 drove his tractor, sporting a large American flag, into a pond adjacent to the Lincoln Memorial in Washington, DC. This action was to protest against cuts in tobacco subsidies. Much was made of reports that he had two bombs in the tractor. These, it later transpired, were RAID-brand 'bug bombs' capable not of exploding, but of releasing fumes lethal to insects in enclosed spaces. Perhaps the most prominent farmer who appears on terrorist databases is José Bové, who came to international attention after using his tractor to dismantle a McDonald's restaurant in the French town of Millau. This political activist, protester and serial dumper of dung sat as a member of the European Parliament in Brussels until 2019.

What is far from a joke is the proliferation of murderous attacks by lone actors who claim to act for ideological reasons as diverse as being an incel (*involuntary celibate*) or saving unborn children from the abortion "holocaust".

In April 2018 a man drove a van onto the pavements of a Toronto street, mowing down pedestrians as he travelled several blocks before being stopped by police. His victims included Beutis Renuka Amarasinghe (forty-five), So He Chung (twenty-two) and Dorothy Sewell (eighty). Despite his attempts to provoke the police into shooting him, going as far as to mime reaching for what he said was his gun, he was captured alive. He had no gun. Immediately before going out to kill, he posted the following on Facebook: "The Incel rebellion has already begun." Naming the lone mass killer who glorified incel culture in a massacre in 2014, he added: "We will overthrow all the Chads and Stacys. All hail the Supreme Gentleman [...]!"

To most of us, at the time, this missive was likely to sound meaningless. Incels are men, usually part of an online community, who blame their status on women whom they label as "evil", "sluts" and "destroyers" who wield too much sexual/romantic power over (heterosexual) men. "Chads and Stacys" are the men and women who have easy access to sex, in contrast to the incels' own self-described undeserved exclusion.

The killer referenced by the Toronto perpetrator was a loner who, in 2014 in Isla Vista, California, went on a murderous rampage, stabbing, shooting and running down twenty people (of whom six died) before shooting himself. The victims included Weihan "David" Wang (twenty-one), Veronika Elizabeth Weiss (nineteen) and Katherine "Katie" Breann Cooper (twenty-three). He left behind videos and documents that raged against women for rejecting and humiliating him. He and his manifesto have become iconic for elements in the incel community. The casualty list from the Toronto attack suggests that women were targeted. Here, an odd ideology that denigrates half the human race was used to justify a massacre intended to end in 'suicide by cop'.

There is debate over whether the 1916 Easter Rising and subsequent Irish Republican Army (IRA) terrorism sped or slowed progress towards establishing an independent Republic of Ireland, and equally, how important the role of terrorist groups such as the Irgun were in establishing the State of Israel. What is not in doubt is that leading members of those terrorist groups, such as Éamonn de Valera and Menachem Begin, were later to rise to positions of leadership, and would come to be acknowledged internationally as worthy representatives of their respective nations. The list of those labelled and prosecuted for terrorist acts include Jomo Kenyatta (leader of the Mau Mau) and African National Congress leader Nelson Mandela, both of whom also went on to become presidents of the countries they had fought to liberate.

These were nationalist movements with substantial support among the population of countries being occupied and administered by a foreign power; that any members of al-Qaeda or Islamic State will one day emerge as respected politicians seems unlikely. Members of terrorist groups take extreme and violent measures to advance their political or religious ideals, but they are usually otherwise functional and sometimes highly talented individuals. They tend to be people who thrive in group situations, rather than being loners. The lone mass killer, by contrast, is almost always an isolate who has little interest in or talent for social and group interaction.

Members of terrorist groups could be regarded as exhibiting a form of social pathology, but they rarely suffer from major psychopathology. Certainly, those I have encountered, who had been active in the Irish republican movement and the Algerian National Liberation Front were, in different ways, very functional, capable people. This picture of a terrorist as someone blessed with good mental health is complicated by the use, in certain currently active terrorist organisations, of psychologically vulnerable and even intellectually impaired people to commit high-risk or suicidal attacks. These people, who are often children or adolescents, are rarely part of the core militant group or cell. They tend to be aspirants to membership enthralled by the idea of becoming like their heroes. (Yet, as the great Irish writer Brendan Behan cautions in his autobiographical book *Borstal Boy* – which recounts his involvement as an adolescent in an IRA bombing campaign – we should not assume that all adolescent terrorists are foolish dupes.)

In 2009 Leon Panetta, then director of the CIA, stated, apropos of terrorism: “It is the lone wolf strategy that I think we have to pay attention to as the main threat to this country.” In the same vein, Eric Holder, US attorney general at the time, claimed: “The thing that keeps me awake most at night is concern about the lone wolf who goes undetected.” Such hyperbole cannot be justified by the number of casualties so far inflicted by lone terrorists, but it does alert us to the fact that the established methods of countering terrorism are of little use against this type of murderer.

The massacre in San Bernardino in 2015, and another in Orlando in 2016, were claimed by their perpetrators to be political acts committed on behalf of extremist organisations. These killers had had little if any direct contact with any terrorist group. The Orlando killer claimed allegiance to both ISIS and Hizbullah, apparently unaware that these groups were violently opposed to each other. The allegiances of the San Bernardino killers were clear and coherent, though they had never had any substantial contact with members of the organisation at whose behest they claim to have acted.

The lone mass killer conceives, plans and accomplishes his murderous project in isolation. Members of terrorist groups cooperate with each other in planning and carrying out their attacks. The loner often intends to die as part of the massacre, whereas terrorist-group members may be willing to die for their cause but usually make some attempt to escape alive (suicide bombers are an obvious exception). The terrorist group acts to promote its cause; the lone-actor massacre is about self-promotion.

By comparison with members of most terrorist organisations, lone killers have significantly more mental-health problems. Security and Crime Science professor Paul Gill and his group found that more than 40 per cent had previous contact with mental-health services, against less than 5 per cent for the others – and that they had more than fifteen times the level of psychotic disorder found in the general population. Other studies support the idea that terrorism plays a secondary role in lone mass killings. The legal scholar Joel Capellán examined 282 lone-actor massacres and found "very similar profiles between those claiming an ideological motivation and the rest". Another study by criminologist Adam Lankford also suggested any differences between the apparently politically motivated lone mass killers and the rest were largely superficial, with both groups sharing a pattern of social marginalisation, family disruption, school and work problems and a precipitating crisis.

Whereas most terrorist groups see themselves as waging a political war on behalf of their community, the perpetrators of lone-terrorist massacres are acting as, and for, some kind of religious or political elite, and against those among whom they live and by whom they have so often felt themselves persecuted and humiliated. The connection between lone mass killings and this kind of elitist political ideology stretches all the way back to Ernst Wagner, who joined the Nazi Party soon after its creation and remained a member until his death. It is doubtful that the party knew its long-term member was incarcerated in an asylum for the criminally insane. Wagner's writings echoed some of the themes in Hitler's *Mein Kampf*, including the preoccupation with degeneration, the weakening of the nation by the spread of syphilis, the loss of the heroic and military virtues and the idea of the decline of the West brought about by the rise of Jewish financiers and capitalists.

In planning their attacks, terrorist groups tend to focus on specific targets that will ideally both generate wide media coverage and express some element of their political agenda. In part, it is about the politics of spectacle, bringing attention to their cause. Lone mass killers, whether or not they claim an ideological motive, focus their planning on making *themselves* the centre of a spectacle: drawing attention to themselves first and foremost.

The terrorist group hopes its actions will speak to supporters and the potentially sympathetic. It intends to frighten and disrupt the lives of those it regards as enemies, and to evoke a violent and disproportionate response from the authorities that will drive the uncommitted sympathiser into their camp. Lone mass killers, by contrast, are addressing an audience made up of those they believe have rejected and persecuted them, although some may dream of becoming a hero to those like themselves. Their message is one of despair and hate directed at the world in general.

Terrorist organisations such as al-Qaeda and Islamic State have become highly sophisticated in using the internet to recruit future lone mass killers to their ranks. The attraction for these recruits is not just the theology and political ideology, but the narrative that is presented to them with consummate skill. It invites them to identify themselves as members of a persecuted and wretched group – all Muslims, as al-Qaeda and Islamic State would have it, especially those living in the

West: *your misery is but one instance of the misery inflicted on us all by Western imperialism*. The other component of this narrative urges the taking on of the role of hero, willing to fight and die to help liberate one's fellow victims. The narrative does not promise merely the useful sacrifice of a soldier, but a hero's death that shall be celebrated and remembered by all those imagined suffering brothers and sisters. Religious martyrdom is thrown in to guarantee manumission of past sins, together with eternal glory.

In short, lone terrorists are largely pursuing a personal agenda of revenge and vindication, driven by their own resentment at the world. Members of terrorist groups may also be driven by personal experiences of injustice and humiliation, but they have sublimated these through identification with the oppression experienced by the population on whose behalf they believe they are struggling. For the lone terrorist, ideology is largely, though not entirely, an excuse for a murderous rampage. For the terrorist group, ideological and religious enthusiasms are the *raison d'être* for these actions. In the end, lone terrorists are exactly that: loners, howling against a world that has failed them personally.

CHAPTER 10

In pursuit of justice denied

ONE DAY, X, an intelligent, articulate young Australian man pursuing a university degree in the humanities decided that after "waking up, having a light breakfast [and] loading my gun", he would be "going out [with the intention] to kill seven or eight people" and "be killed by police". This story is based on the evidence and reports I and others presented at his trial.

X had entered his former workplace armed with a handgun, and opened fire. One person was killed, and two injured; more would have perished had not others present courageously run at him, wresting the gun from his hands and restraining him until the police arrived to take him into custody. Any doubts about X's intentions were dispelled by the statement he subsequently made to the police:

> I intended to go and wreak great vengeance ... I was hoping to kill seven or eight people, but unfortunately I didn't get around to that, and I was hoping to be killed by one of you people. I didn't get around to that either, so I fucked up completely.

When the police searched the killer's apartment after the shooting, they found what amounted to a manifesto attempting to justify his actions. This included the lines:

> I am not crazy. I tried every legal way possible to find justice for being wronged. This is a warning to employers, politicians, and corrupt men of authority, the little guy is getting tired of getting used and shat upon with no avenue for fair play. Cry havoc and let slip the dogs of war.

This man had, over the years, often found himself in conflict with those around him. When confronted, his usual response had been to back down rather than pursue his complaints. Entering university as a mature student, he resolved not to continue merely accepting the injustices inflicted on him, but to fight back. He began planning the attack after a particularly galling series of adverse findings by agencies such as the Fair Work Commission, Equal Opportunity and the State Ombudsman, to which he had complained about wrongful dismissal from a restaurant at which he had worked part-time. He later explained that this failure by organisations that should have supported his 'pursuit of justice' left him no alternative but to take justice into his own hands.

X was sensitive to any slight or apparent lack of respect. He was constantly alert to any hint that his rights and prerogatives were being infringed. He did not seem to accord much respect to the rights and prerogatives of others – though he seems to have taken the view that by pursuing his own complaints, he was fighting on behalf of those less able or willing to stand up for themselves. In prison, he styled himself a spokesman for the ostensible grievances of his fellow inmates. Unsurprisingly, this did not endear him to prison officers, against whom most of his complaints were directed. Less predictable was the extent of the dislike he evoked in some of the other prisoners, who seem to have regarded him as meddling in their business.

X sought to present his workplace attack as the result of a quest for justice, both for himself and for those he supposed to be other victims. He claimed that he was not really responsible for the killing and wounding because his actions had been forced upon him by persecution and exclusion – of him, as well as all the 'little people' like him. This excuse needs to be examined.

His claims of having been a victim of malevolence and frank persecution throughout his life were not based on delusional experiences such as those found in psychotic illnesses of a schizophrenic type. Delusions of persecution in such conditions usually revolve around sufferers feeling targeted by some group (the CIA, the Freemasons, etc.), with the experience of being constantly observed both by electronic means and spies. There is also the perception of plots to physically harm them, as well as threats conveyed in code (easily comprehensible to them, if obscure to others). X had had no such experiences. He was convinced that his persecution was a product of an inherently unfair society that had failed to recognise his manifest merits. He was sure he had been targeted out of envy and misunderstanding. His resentment at the treatment he had received over the years did not form the basis for any coherent political position, though he did identify himself with others whom he believed had been similarly disadvantaged. In the end, his resentment was first and foremost about *himself*, with the added conceit of acting on behalf of a similarly oppressed and excluded population. In his mind he was a leader; in reality, he was a self-appointed leader of an army unaware or indifferent to his very existence.

X constantly experienced himself as being the object of others' consideration. Words half-overheard, possible glances in his direction, laughter from across the room, people walking past him in the street: in each and every encounter was the possibility of malevolent or disparaging attention.

In attempting to understand the internal world of someone who has committed a terrible crime, it is important not to endow perfectly normal mental mechanisms with a pathological, sinister significance. The self-conscious adolescent, for example, is often troubled by the thought that others will notice every pimple, every awkward gesture, every stumbled sentence. For some, the experience of adolescence includes feeling transparent to the gaze of others who, it is imagined, are able to divine their innermost shameful and embarrassing secrets. Such experiences can last a lifetime for those cursed with shyness, who may never escape the belief that they are noticed and judged by other people. Shy individuals may well understand intellectually that people around them are mainly uninterested in anything but themselves; but this offers little comfort to them as they squirm nonetheless, unnoticed by the passing multitude.

The tendency to oversensitivity in X was more pronounced than could be explained by shyness or some hangover from adolescence. His experience of others' supposed attentions had a different quality. He did not feel *embarrassed* by the supposed attention, he felt *attacked*. The shy and the adolescent experience the intrusive interest of others as a product of their own inadequacies. By contrast, X experienced attention as a product of the malevolence of others, in no small part generated by their envious awareness of his superior abilities and intellect. In short, oversensitivity and self-referentiality in him was morbid in its pervasiveness; it distorted his ability to understand other people and their actual intentions.

He prided himself on being well organised and never leaving a job unfinished. Exploring further, it became clear that he had traits of rigidity and obsessiveness. He did not have an obsessional illness: far from resisting his tendency to repeatedly check and rigidly insist on 'proper' procedures, he regarded these tendencies as virtues.

He was not shy or self-effacing; nor was he a man with modest pretensions. He was, in his eyes, a superior being, furious at having been held down by misunderstanding and injustice. He was a failure – not as a result of any inadequacies, but because of the ill will of others. He was, above all, a *victim*. It was as a victim bent on revenge against individuals and society at large that he set out that day to kill and maim.

X was somewhat unusual for a lone mass killer. He was not interested, let alone obsessed, with guns. The handgun he used was purchased illegally a few days before the attack. Violent films and shoot-up video games played no part in his recreational activities:

contemporary fiction and poetry occupied a more central place. As an adolescent, he had reluctantly gone hunting with his father and brother, but it was many years since he had handled any firearms. His denials that he was at all prone to indulging in extended fantasies of heroic last stands were convincing. He acknowledged only brief, angry impulses to attack people whom he believed had insulted or disadvantaged him. X had never harboured military ambitions; his only contact with a vaguely related organisation involved brief membership in a volunteer country fire brigade.

He had some knowledge of previous lone-actor massacres, but only in the same way that most people would have known about them. He denied ever seeking details about the perpetrators or the events themselves. Unlike so many lone mass killers, he was not a lifelong social isolate. He had had friends, though none in recent years with whom he was sufficiently close as to be able to confide in or seek support from. His social circle at the time of the attack was made up of an ever-changing group of people with whom he met casually in gatherings, augmented by the occasional coworker. On his university course he had made no real friends among fellow students, probably in part because he was twenty years older than most of them. He had had girlfriends and, on more than one occasion in the past, had even cohabited for a time, but these relationships ended after a matter of months because, he said, of a mutual recognition that they weren't working out. It had been some years since he had had an extended emotional and sexual relationship.

What was the bridge between the failure of his claims for wrongful dismissal and the homicidal violence perpetrated by this apparently rather unlikely lone mass killer? Loss of the job and the context in which it occurred was, for him, a particularly devastating experience. He had worked there for a considerable length of time, and fondly believed he was an outstanding member of staff valued by management and coworkers. He understood that he might have upset management on occasion by his insistence on what he deemed proper practices and procedures, but from his perspective the contribution he'd made to the smooth running of the business should have outweighed any friction. One aspect of his dismissal that caused particular distress was that he received no support from coworkers. To compound the insult, he later learnt that management had claimed his dismissal had arisen on account of dishonesty – this, in the case of a man who prided himself on honesty in all things.

The job provided X with funds to support his studies. He was then in the midst of his second year, and had obtained good grades. The hoped-for degree would, he believed, enable him to lift himself out of a life working in unskilled and semi-skilled jobs, all too often on a short-term or casual basis. The degree was to be the door into a world in which his intellectual abilities and personal qualities would finally find recognition. The loss of the job and the circumstances of his dismissal put all his dreams for the future in jeopardy.

It had been a long road to finally entering university in his late thirties. During his upbringing, the only reading material likely to be found at home consisted of magazines about sport or cars – areas in which he lacked the enthusiasm and skills of his father and brothers. By his account, he had never been particularly close to any of them, but he had never been bullied or mistreated by them, either. Similarly, his mother was caring and concerned, if somewhat distant emotionally. He grew up *in* the family, but was never entirely *of* the family.

His life at school was similar. For the most part, he was ignored by his peers. He was an overweight, physically awkward, shy child who neither wished to join in other children's activities, nor was particularly welcome to do so. At times, during his progress through the school system, he did have like-minded friends, but none of these bonds continued into adult life. He seems to have suffered more than his fair share of bullying.

When his IQ was assessed after his arrest, it was found to be in the superior range, but this does not seem to have been recognised either in his family or by his teachers; nor did it manifest in any academic success during his childhood and adolescence. One possible curse in childhood is to be surrounded by peers and adults who are not at your level of intellectual ability: your capacities will go unrecognised and undeveloped, and you will never be confronted with those of similar or greater ability. X grew up an autodidact with an unstructured, uneven knowledge of the areas in which he took interest, unchallenged by intellects from whom he might have learned and who might have induced a greater element of modesty about his high – but not stellar – abilities. The modern university, with its vast classes and smorgasbord of study options, rarely does much to rescue such feral intellects – but it can offer a life raft of sorts, as in this case.

The loss of the job sank his life raft. That it generated distress and rage is understandable, but where did a plan come from for a mass murder in which he planned to die among his victims?

After a particularly galling interaction that leaves one humiliated and, for whatever reason, unable to adequately respond, which of us has not indulged in dreaming up the ripostes that would have turned the tables to our advantage? *If only I'd thought of saying that or dared to do the other.* Unlike X, most of us do not let such episodes continue to rankle, regularly retrieving the memories, rekindling the experience of hurt. When questioned, it became clear that he rarely, if ever, turned to fantasy to remove the sting by retrospectively reframing the experience. On the contrary, he effectively *relived* the experience repeatedly. Listening to his stories of humiliation, in many instances it was not at all clear from the account of what had been said and done that the supposed antagonist had had any malicious intent. The perceived offence came from X's assumptions about the other's sentiments at the time and from what he assumed was a widespread antagonism just waiting for a chance to surface. For X, resentment was not just an experience attached to some specific events but had become the dominant attitude towards the world.

He seemed to regard himself as more sinned-against than sinning. On several occasions over the time I was seeing him, I made gentle attempts to remind him that he was in prison facing one charge of murder and several of attempted murder – and that as a result of his actions, people were grieving and others were in pain both physical and mental. Sometimes he simply ignored me and continued expressing his personal grievances; at others, he gave what seemed a formal response: he was terribly sorry for what he had done. Although appropriate enough in its content, this appeared to lack any emotional commitment. In the end, I decided this was not callousness but an attempt to distance himself from the horror of that day and hurry on to less disturbing topics.

It is far from uncommon for those who have killed someone to blot out the memory by forgetting the actual event, even while accepting they were responsible for committing it. More problematic are those who claim they carried out the killing in a state in which they were not really themselves – that there was a separation between their conscious mind and the actions of their body. They were, in short, dissociated, and no more responsible than if they had been asleep at the time. Some of my less sceptical colleagues offer this as a defence, ignoring that, in states of high arousal from fear or rage, the out-of-body experience with an apparent slowing of time and sense of distancing from reality is not uncommon – in fact, it can be *functional*. What was unusual about X was that he had a clear memory of the events themselves, but a rather childlike reluctance to contemplate the implications of those events in the here and now.

His first contact with mental-health services had occurred five years before the attack, following a suicide attempt. He had tried to kill himself after the breakdown of what was to be his last close relationship with a woman. The medical records indicate that this was a determined attempt that he survived by chance, rather than intention. He was briefly hospitalised, but, surprisingly, there was no psychiatric evaluation, though he was offered an appointment with the mental-health services that he declined to attend. For an articulate man capable of showing a degree of psychological insight, he was remarkably unforthcoming about his state of mind prior to, and following, this suicide attempt. He assured me the decision to kill himself had been perfectly reasonable given the situation in which he found himself: unpartnered, with no real friends, no job prospects and little chance of rectifying these deficiencies. The reason he gave for not making a second attempt was fatalism: he accepted that he was destined to survive. In the aftermath of this suicide attempt, he began seriously considering studying for a university degree. He claimed he was always on the moody side and prone to anxiety, particularly with new people, but he denied most of the disturbances usually associated with significant levels of depression prior to the attempt.

He made another serious suicide attempt following the loss of his job at the restaurant. He was then seen by a student counsellor on a number of occasions over the next few months. The history he provided for these sessions was of distress and lowered mood for months prior to this attempt. In counselling, the ongoing conflict over his job loss was a central focus. He was obsessed with obtaining some kind of compensation for wrongful dismissal. Mixed in his plans to pursue complaints against his erstwhile employers were vague hints both of trying to kill himself and of violent retribution. The therapist made appropriate enquiries to clarify his suicidal and violent propensities, but X was able to reassure her he had no intentions of acting on these thoughts. The suggestions of violence emerged in part through his report of hearing voices encouraging him to take murderous revenge. A psychiatrist also saw him during this period as part of an assessment of a worker's compensation claim. In this interview, he spoke as well of voices over the previous weeks telling him to kill himself along with others who had persecuted him.

In the context of what was to occur, the references both to being suicidal and potentially being homicidal take on a particularly sinister significance. At the time, such hints – even direct threats – suggesting suicidal or homicidal tendencies may not have seemed of great concern, as they were not considered to indicate any real commitment to acting. In this case, both professionals attempted to explore whether or not X was seriously considering killing himself or others. They took reassurance on both counts from his denials. They would likely have been more anxious about threats of suicide, given X's history, than of homicide: he had no known history of violence.

Mental-health professionals in general are reasonably good at assessing suicide risk, but often poor at weighting threats of violence. The clinical notes from these two professionals suggest that they were no worse than most at addressing the possibility of violence.

So how did an intelligent man who took pleasure in literature, and whose hopes were pinned on obtaining a degree in the humanities, finish up a murderer? The answer is not to be found in any one factor: not in any obsession with guns, or lax gun laws, or psychiatric illness (though he was far from a paragon of mental health), or ideological or theological enthusiasm. It was a lethal combination of circumstances: vulnerabilities of personality; an intense sense of grievance; suicidal despair; a grandiosity that could only understand failure in terms of persecution; and markedly obsessive personality traits, ensuring that once he'd committed to his plan for murder-suicide, X was likely to pursue it to its conclusion.

The good news – if those are the words to use about a tragedy that killed one man, injured others and destroyed the life of the perpetrator – is that multiple factors, none of them in itself sufficient, imply multiple ways in which such tragedies can be prevented in the future. The message is that this could have been prevented had the knowledge, and the procedures to apply that knowledge, been present at the time.

CHAPTER 11

A Norwegian tragedy

THE MASSACRE THAT occurred on the Norwegian island of Utøya in 2011 claimed more lives than any lone-actor massacre before it, though this terrible toll was to be exceeded the 2016 Nice truck massacre. Among those killed were Birgitte Smetbak (fifteen), Gunnar Linakar (twenty-two) and Carina Borgund (seventeen). The importance of this event is not simply a matter of the number of people killed, but of the three fundamental questions it raised. The first is the relationship of this type of mass murder to terrorism. The second is the role of psychotic illness in such events. And the third is the recurring question of what sort of person can commit such an atrocity. Our enquiry into these events is aided by the extensive court documents. Whatever the wisdom of allowing the murderer to be tried in open court before the world's media, it did generate a mass of evidence about the man, all of which is now available.

On 22 July 2011, a thirty-two-year-old Norwegian man carried out two attacks. The first involved a 450-kilogram bomb placed in a parked van in an area of Oslo that was home to several government buildings, including the office of the prime minister. After setting a timer on the bomb fuse, the man walked a couple of hundred metres to his other vehicle, which he had parked some hours previously. The bomb exploded at about 3.30 PM, killing eight people and seriously injuring nine. The man was, by this time, already driving out of Oslo towards Tyrifjorden, in which lies the island of Utøya. It was here that a youth camp organised by the Norwegian Labour Party was in progress.

Parking his van near the jetty, the man began waiting for the next ferry to Utøya island. It was cancelled because of an alert sent out when it became known that a bomb had exploded in Oslo. Despite this, the killer, who was dressed in a semblance of a police uniform, persuaded the crew to transport him, plus his automatic rifle and handgun, over the few hundred metres to the island. He arrived on the island at about 5.15 PM. The shootings that followed left sixty-nine dead and thirty-three injured, many seriously. The killer is described as walking steadily around the island, deliberately shooting at the young people who were running in all directions to try to escape.

Armed police finally arrived at the island about an hour later. They soon found the killer, who, on being challenged, set his rifle down against a nearby tree and surrendered. He made no effort to engage the police in a firefight. Subsequently he claimed that he had expected to be shot by police and die among his victims. In fact, when he saw police advancing, he meekly surrendered, making no attempt to bring about his own death. Those killed were mainly adolescents, the youngest being just fourteen years old.

The extensive archive available on the man and the massacre includes documents from the trial, among which are psychiatric and psychological reports as well as the court transcripts. Among several books on the subject, perhaps the best to date is *One of Us* by Åsne Seierstad.

The Utøya killer's parents were an ill-matched couple. His father was a university graduate who served in the Norwegian diplomatic service. His mother had received only a basic education, and was from a disorganised and disadvantaged family. When the couple met, she and her six-year-old daughter from a previous relationship were living on welfare. The parents both seem to have had a talent for establishing relationships, but neither seems to have been able to maintain them long-term. The killer's father would go on to have four marriages, and his mother a number of semi-permanent partnerships. The parents separated when the future murderer was still a toddler. At the time they were living in London, where his father was on the staff of the Norwegian embassy. The boy and his mother returned to Oslo.

The next three years of the boy's life were marked by chaos. His mother appears to have had considerable trouble coping, despite support from both the welfare and mental-health services. The reports prepared on the boy at the time by child-protection service workers suggest that much of the day-to-day care fell to his elder half-sister. He was placed into short-term foster care on several occasions.

When he began attending preschool, his behaviour was so disturbed that he was, at the age of four, referred to a centre for child and adolescent psychiatry. He was described as a socially isolated child who took no joy in life. He neither joined in games with other children, nor seemed to play with toys by himself. There are also notes from his preschool about aggressive behaviour towards other children, and being clingy towards staff, and dependent on them. The child psychiatrist and the child psychologist who assessed him around this time were sufficiently concerned to recommend that the boy be removed from his mother's care and placed in a foster home. This did not occur, in part because the father seems to have intervened. There are similarities between the descriptions of the future killer at this time and those recorded about the Port Arthur killer at a similar age. The subsequent progress of the two was, however, very different.

As the years passed, the boy's behaviour at school became less disruptive, and concern about the home situation seems to have dissipated. This pause may have reflected improvements in his mother's mental health, and the fact that she obtained stable accommodation and greater financial security. It may also have been a result of his father's having begun to take a somewhat more active role in supporting the family, and at least seeing his son during holidays. From this time, during school holidays, he visited his father, who now lived in France with his next wife.

By the time he moved on to the local secondary school, he seems to have become an unremarkable boy who was academically average, had friends his own age and behaved no better or worse than his peers. In secondary school he began spending much of his time with a group of three friends, one of whom was the son of Pakistani immigrants. The group shared a fondness for hip-hop music and dressed in the outsize, low-hanging jeans favoured by their musician heroes. At this stage in his life, far from harbouring obvious racist tendencies, he socialised with boys from diverse ethnic backgrounds who were first- or second-generation immigrants.

In his early teens, the boy, together with his three close friends, developed an enthusiasm for spray-painting graffiti on walls and other suitable surfaces. Tagging had become a popular pastime for young people in Oslo, and had spawned a subculture complete with its own hierarchies and competing factions. It took two basic forms: street art in the mode of Banksy, and taggers who derived their approach mainly from the territory markers of US street gangs. The boy came to see himself as a major force in the tagging community – but his pretensions caused him to be ridiculed and ultimately rejected. His response appears to have been to redouble his efforts at tagging, which resulted in his arrest on three occasions. These led to no criminal sanctions, but they did incur a punitive response from his father, who not only stopped having his son visit for holidays but also ceased all contact. The fifteen-year-old was, from this point on, totally rejected by his father, with whom he would have further contact on only one occasion, by phone.

The boy's days as a self-proclaimed rebel and tagger came to an end when he moved from secondary school to an upper school, and left his three friends behind. In the new school, he found that his classmates came predominately from prosperous backgrounds far removed from those of his erstwhile companions. He was apparently able to reinvent himself, discarding the garb of the 'ghetto outcast' for the polo necks and slacks of the young bourgeoisie. Those who knew him at this time imply that he swapped his working-class accent for something closer to the educated tones of his father. Now he boasted of being a born entrepreneur on his way to his first millions. He seems to have been able to keep up with the lifestyle of his new and far more affluent social group by working part-time as a telephone salesman. He did not complete his schooling and go on to university with most of his peer group, but moved to working full-time to acquire money to launch his first business venture.

He joined Norway's Progress Party at the age of eighteen. The party espouses politics typical of European right-wing populist movements: ultra-nationalist, anti-immigration, anti-global capitalism, pro-small business, tough on crime, anti-welfare state, pro-strong government, anti-trade union, pro-military and committed to the far right's take on the traditional social and family values of a Christian society.

Scandinavia is usually regarded as dominated by liberal and social-democratic ideas, rather than by politics associated with right-wing, authoritarian, nationalist movements. Åsne Seierstad, in her excellent book, goes to some lengths to place the Utøya killer and the massacre in the context of the Norwegian political scene. This makes it all the more extraordinary that she can write that Norway's Labour Party had been running the country virtually without a break from 1935 until 1981 – eliding the years 1942–45, when Norway was ruled by the Vidkun Quisling-led government that not only collaborated with the Nazis but also actively imitated them in many ways. Norway, on a per-capita basis, provided more recruits to the Waffen SS than almost any other nation. It was also the only Scandinavian country to mount a serious military opposition to the Nazis, however, both in the resistance at home and the free Norwegian forces abroad, for which it paid a heavy price in the form of reprisals.

(Seierstad's momentary slip into forgetfulness is not atypical for Norwegians of her generation. I remember, during a visit to Norway, a gathering of my wife's family, during which I conversed with one of her cousins. He was a lecturer in history who spoke at length, and with considerable feeling, about the extent to which the deep divisions in

Norway exposed during the war were now being glossed over while, in his view, remaining unresolved. It was his view that, just below the surface, there continues to be a current of extreme right-wing political and cultural ideas in today's Norway. When the massacre at Utøya occurred, I was reminded of his warning that Norway could one day pay dearly for failing to confront honestly what he termed the fascist strain both in its past and its present.)

The young man threw himself into his membership of the Progressive Party. He worked hard at all those mundane tasks that party workers must perform to recruit new members and garner support. He took on thankless tasks such as distributing leaflets, selling party publications and organising local meetings. He made no secret of his ambition to ascend to the highest ranks of the party, and hoped to stand as one of its parliamentary candidates. Its influence was growing, and it had polled some 20 per cent of votes in a recent national election. A political career in the party must have seemed to the man a very real possibility.

He met and formed a relationship with another recent recruit to the party – she was in fact ethnically South Asian, and had been adopted by a Norwegian couple when still an infant. She identified strongly with Norway, and believed that all immigrants were obliged to adopt the customs and culture of their new country. Whatever else this young woman brought to the relationship with him, she introduced her own enthusiasm for shooting and for the military, of which she had been a member as a cadet. According to her, when she met the future murderer, he had already had an interest in guns and considerable knowledge about different aspects of the weapons. The two of them became members of an Oslo gun club, where they practised target shooting. The nature and extent of their relationship is not entirely clear from the various accounts.

The man's sexuality seems somewhat uncertain. A number of people who had known him expressed the view that he was probably gay. He had described himself on one occasion as "metrosexual", by which he meant a heterosexual who enjoyed putting on makeup and wearing clothes that were flamboyant, if not necessarily feminine. He is known to have made at least one attempt to acquire a wife. In 2004 he contacted a young woman from Belarus through an internet matchmaking service. She came to Oslo to stay with him for a time; the relationship seems to have quite rapidly soured, and she returned home. In the five years or so before the killings, he had no lasting sexual or intimate relationships or even, as far as is known, brief sexual encounters.

He made considerable efforts to ingratiate himself with the Progressive Party hierarchy. This seems to have been less than entirely successful. Some in the leadership group have, in retrospect, claimed they found him a boastful and irritating young man more interested in his personal advancement than in the party and its ideology. The man, however, appears to have been confident at the time that he would soon receive the call to join the party's list of potential parliamentary candidates. In this, he was to be disappointed. The setback must have been aggravated by the fact that his girlfriend was the one who was asked to join the inner group of the party's parliamentarians-in-waiting. Following the frustration of his ambitions, his involvement in Progressive Party activities gradually waned.

His would-be political career might have languished, but his entrepreneurial activities increased. He made several attempts to start up companies, though most failed at an early stage. He had one real success: a venture based on selling facsimiles of educational certificates and university degrees. His little company manufactured such documents, and sold them over the internet. They were made out in the name specified by the purchaser and came complete with authentic-looking seals and signatures. A thin veil of legitimacy was maintained by advertising these documents as copies for use as decorations or props for theatrical performances.

He appears to have made a considerable amount of money from this scam, and was able to move into an apartment in a desirable area of Oslo favoured by young professionals. The money was sufficient for him to create an aura of success; but in 2005 the venture was shut down, probably in response to an increasing interest being shown by the police.

He next set himself up as a trader on the stock exchange, but his share acquisitions, far from increasing his wealth, left him almost penniless. This newfound poverty forced him to give up his apartment and the lifestyle he had been enjoying. At the age of twenty-seven, he returned to live with his mother.

At this point in his life, the man was evidently a very different kind of person from most of the perpetrators of lone mass killings described so far in this book. He had gone through a troubled early childhood, but his later progress through primary and secondary school did not mark him out as particularly different from most of his peers. He does seem to have been bumptious and bombastic, but was far from being a social outcast. He had in fact established a wide circle of acquaintances, and maintained a number of close friendships.

His ability to establish long-term friendships is attested to by the number of people who attempted to keep contact with him through the subsequent years of radical isolation. After the massacre, one of his long-term friends spoke of her memory of him as a younger man: outgoing and entertaining, someone perhaps prone to hogging the limelight but not unpleasant or standoffish. She described him in the period after 2004 as having become odd, disconnected and dismissive of attempts to engage in conversation, let alone any social activity.

One key difference between the Utøya killer and most of the cases described in this book is the extent of his involvement in politics. Some of the massacres I have previously cited were perpetrated by men who entertained an interest in politics, often of an extreme right-wing variety. But their engagement rarely extended further than reading. The Utøya killer not only joined a political party, but participated fully in its social and group activities. Even the somewhat antisocial and anarchic taggers he had previously associated with formed groups with their own social and cultural agendas. Thus the Utøya killer, for all his difficulties, could, up to 2004, have been described as a socially active young man able to join with others in political and cultural movements.

In 2004 he effectively withdrew permanently from the outside world, living as a recluse in his mother's apartment. For the next two to three years his days were largely spent within the four walls of his bedroom, sitting before his computer. His life was to merge into that of "Andersnordic", his avatar in *World of Warcraft* and related gaming environments. (As a young friend of mine remarked to me, *World of Warcraft* allows players, even those without much talent, to feel important and to be in charge of many fellow gamers.)

He is known to have spent up to sixteen hours a day living as "Andersnordic" in the gaming spaces. Seierstad, in her book, suggests that these activities were some kind of tonic for his depression. She also draws parallels between his career as "Andersnordic", the warrior of cyberspace, and his previous efforts to establish himself first as a tagger, then as a politician and finally as an entrepreneur. The same route seems to have been followed from obsessive commitment through to demands for recognition as a leading figure and finally to descent into angry resentment when the celebrity he felt was his due failed to materialise. In the gaming world, once again, his search for recognition and admiration had run well ahead of his accumulation of actual accomplishments.

(It is not unusual to observe people expending more effort on establishing and maintaining a reputation than on producing any actual work that might justify this self-proclaimed distinction. And it is tempting to determine, in our present culture, an encouragement to place the appearance of excellence first and foremost. But perhaps it was ever thus.)

Again and again, this solitary man became a celebrity in his own mind, only to find that he remained for others nothing more than a self-aggrandising aspirant. And this was exactly how his years of climbing the gaming hierarchies ended: in resentment and rage at the collapse of another attempt to become famous and admired.

He was now to launch a final quest for fame and significance. He emerged from the world of computer gaming to plunge immediately back into another region of the internet, one occupied by extreme nationalist, religious and racist ideologies. The websites of the radical right glory in such names as *Gates of Vienna*, *Stormfront* and *Atlas Shrugs*. The FBI and anti-terrorist organisations have drawn attention to the risks attending right-wing extremism and the role the internet plays in proselytising for such groups, but this has never evoked media interest to the same extent as Islamic extremism.

In attempting to ascertain the relative contribution of the Utøya killer's political ideology as opposed to his personal psychopathology, it is important to consider how close his expressed ideas were to the orthodoxy of the extreme right. The main source for understanding his ideas is the manifesto he placed on the internet on the day of the mass killings. The statements and rants he was permitted to indulge in during his trial are a further source for understanding what he claimed had motivated his killing and maiming of so many of his fellow citizens.

The manifesto has been used in attempts to demonstrate that he either was, or was not, insane. The document has been termed a "compendium", which in many ways describes it more accurately than *manifesto*. It is a 1,800-page collection of essays, quotations, instructions and political rants interspersed with highly personal disclosures. Commentators have tended to select sentences to fit whatever case they are advancing about this man's nature. Understandably, given its length and structural complexity, there have been few attempts to analyse the document as a whole.

He wrote his compendium in English, not in Norwegian, in the hope of having a wider audience. He apologises in the preamble for any failures in clarity that may thereby have resulted. This modest apology to his future readers is followed by a far from self-effacing series of claims in terms of the work being "truly unique" and the product of "thousands of hours of study". He estimates that he has expended 317,000 euros in its production, mostly accounted for by his time spent on it. The compendium, he writes, "is the most comprehensive database of solution-oriented materials".

The Utøya killer is an autodidact who has learned from his reading, without the guidance and structure that a decent education might have provided. His compendium has both the faults, and to some extent the virtues, of many of the self-taught. He often fails to understand the historical and intellectual context of the subjects about which he writes. On the other hand, he is certainly not hampered by the influence of the assumptions that structure more pedestrian academic discourse. Autodidacts can tend to become caught up in enthusiasm about ideas acquired in what is often a selective and superficial course of study. His greatest problem, however, is common to the age: that of gathering masses of information from websites, many of which are unreliable, and some of which trade in pronouncements that lack the support of anything approaching verifiable evidence.

The document falls into a number of sections, the first of which is a critique of "cultural Marxism", which he regards as today's pervasive political correctness. He traces it back to the writings of Georg Lukács, a Hungarian intellectual and political activist from the early part of the twentieth century perhaps best known for a work of literary criticism, *History and Class Consciousness*. He then moves into a critique of the loose collective of German intellectuals, established first in the 1930s, known as the Frankfurt School. Among the members of this group were luminaries such as Theodor Adorno, Herbert Marcuse and Eric Fromm.

Why he should have spent so much time attacking this particular group is difficult to understand. Even when the group was active, knowledge of the works of its associates was largely confined to socialists opposed to Stalinism and the authoritarianism that bedevilled European communist parties. He references several books by members of the Frankfurt School as well as scholarly works on their ideas. It is difficult to know whether he had ever read these works, or had just read about them on the internet. It is easy to identify errors of fact in his account – for example, the psychoanalyst Wilhelm Reich was not a member of the group. The murderer's critique of the Frankfurt School, for all its simplifications and misunderstandings, does make the case for this group supporting all the things that he detests. They were indeed a group of humanists, socialists, internationalists and anti-racists.

So why did he spend so much time and devote so much space to attacking writers who would be unknown to almost all of his potential readers? I believe this was an attempt to establish at the very beginning of his compendium that he had the credentials of a serious intellectual versed in the history of ideas. Another factor may have been his preoccupation with events in the aftermath of the Second World War, when the seeds were sown for what he regarded as today's European cultural crisis.

This first section of his writings is the most coherent and clearly expressed. Subsequent sections become increasingly verbose and poorly structured. In his multiple attacks on Islam, he makes extensive use of quotes drawn from a remarkably wide range of sources. At one point he writes: "We will revolt against the Nazis of our time, the cultural Marxist multicultural elites ... who are selling us into Muslim slavery." In this statement, as in several other places in the compendium, he attempts to distance himself and his supposed supporters from National Socialism and fascism.

In the rambling, increasingly disorganised sections on Islam, he declares the Crusades wars of self-defence and places responsibility on Muslims for slavery both today and in the past. On page 810 he recaps his accusations directed at Muslims and concludes: "A new era has come, and I hereby declare a pre-emptive war on them." He then predicts that the year 2083 is when the Muslim "menace" will be totally defeated; this explains why he titled his compendium *2083: A European Declaration of Independence*.

In the next thousand or so pages, any semblance of an overarching political argument is lost. The writing becomes more personalised, not only in terms of *I know this* and *I did this* but also replete with autobiographical asides and inappropriate personal revelations. An example of the latter is a discussion of his belief that his mother and half-sister suffer from sexually transmitted diseases, and have "shamed me and shame society".

In noting the loss of clear connections between the topics in the later sections of the compendium, I do not wish to imply that the language used had become disturbed in the manner sometimes encountered in the writings of those with schizophrenic illnesses. If anything, several of the later sections in the compendium, if taken alone, have a greater degree of focus and organisation. We are, for example, treated to a lengthy detailing of body armour and appropriate weaponry that might be used in the coming struggle. (These sections, in all their pedantic detail, bear remarkable similarity to the lists and descriptions of weapons and armour found in the manuals of fantasy games such as *Dungeons & Dragons* and *World of Warcraft*. The shared fantasy world of wargamers has been plucked from online and dropped straight into the Utøya killer's personal world, in which he is planning his actual murderous attack.)

One of the most difficult parts of the compendium to interpret deals with what the killer calls "the European national military commands and the Knights Templars", whom he asserts were refounded when he visited London in 2002. Extensive information is provided about the supposed history of this order of chivalry (the name in fact refers to a medieval military order within Catholicism, which disbanded in the early 1300s). He describes every imaginable aspect of their dress and rituals. These newly formed Knights Templar, he claims, consist of cells spread throughout Europe, each led by what he calls a "Justicar Knight", of which he is one, if not *the* one.

There is a curious moment in the compendium when its author looks forward to a possible trial after completing the massacre he is planning. Here he sets out the role he expects to be played by an attorney in defending a resistance fighter like himself. His requirements include the advocate's willingness to "facilitate you ideologically" and, in particular, to "assure that you are able to read your statement and build your case against the regime". In the event, the Norwegian legal system, if not his lawyers, cooperated fully in allowing him to do exactly what he had laid out in this document.

The last few hundred pages of the compendium are undoubtedly the strangest. The killer gives us a detailed account of his preparations for the massacre, interspersed with what amounts to a daily diary that not only gives details of what he is currently doing but also digresses into aspects of his personal history. One section is written in the form of an interview in which an imagined journalist poses questions such as, "Can you describe your childhood?" Here, boasting and general puffery are interspersed with attempts to adopt a self-deprecatory tone, as when he writes, "I am generally perceived as quite arrogant" and "I have a relatively inflated ego with a constant need to feed on an intellectual level."

In this part of the compendium, he describes in detail his struggles to produce the bombs he will later detonate in the centre of Oslo. I doubt that anyone could follow the bomb-making instructions he provides here, even if they could separate them from the parallel account of each and every thought and action that occurred as an accompaniment to his making of the explosives. At one point he shares with the reader that "I downloaded all seven seasons of the [TV series] *The Shield*", which he assures us he enjoyed watching. He goes on to list other recommended TV series. The compendium thus ends with this increasingly odd conflation of minutely described preparations for the killings with what amounts to a banal "Dear Diary ..."

The Norwegian courts operate on the inquisitorial system common to continental Europe rather than the adversarial system found in the English-speaking world. The killer's trial began with the court appointing two psychiatrists to report on whether or not he was psychotic. Under Norwegian law, a person found to be psychotic at the time of committing a criminal act is unconditionally exempt from punishment even if the offence is not a direct result of the psychosis. The court can order that such offenders be compulsorily detained in a mental-health facility, usually until such time as their mental disorder is in remission and they are assessed as presenting no continuing threat to members of the community.

The central criterion for diagnosing someone as psychotic in Norwegian law is *the serious impairment of the offender's ability to make a realistic assessment of their relationship to the surrounding world*. The law avoids any specific criteria beyond this rather vague requirement. At least in theory, the decision depends on the evidence of the mental-health professionals, with the judge ideally playing a relatively minor role. The two experts appointed by the court, Dr Synne Husby and Dr Torgeir Sørheim, reported that the Utøya killer was indeed psychotic and, by implication, exempt from punishment.

The terms *responsible*, *culpable* and *punishable* all amount to the same thing, despite many theoretical discussions in legal texts about the distinctions. In Norway, in the usual run of things, the experts' opinions would have settled the matter. All that would remain to be done was to hold the briefest of trials before the defendant was committed to a secure psychiatric facility.

The killer was furious when he learned of the psychiatrists' opinions, and demanded that his lawyers challenge their findings. He wanted a full trial with the opportunity to perform before the world media. In and of themselves, neither his views on the matter nor those of his lawyers were of interest to the court. However, the opinion from the first two experts was leaked to the press, which created a massive public outcry.

As so often happens, the general public – encouraged by elements in the media – confused the finding of 'not legally responsible because of psychosis' with the offender 'getting away with the crime', or even 'being set free'. In reality, someone who has committed homicide or another serious crime and is found insane or mentally impaired is *not* released, but incarcerated – often for as long as, or longer than, they would have been had they been found guilty. The only real difference is whether they are detained in a secure mental-health facility or a prison. In this case, it is difficult to imagine any future government ever allowing the Utøya killer's release, even if they had to change the law to ensure that he remained in detention. (Just such a change in the law occurred in 2014 in Australia to prevent the release of the perpetrator of the Hoddle Street massacre.)

The court in this case, however, acceded to popular and possibly political pressure by appointing two additional mental-health experts, Dr Terje Tørrissen and Dr Agnar Aspaas, to evaluate the Utøya killer. They concluded that he was *not* psychotic, creating a situation in which a full trial now became inevitable, unless he were to plead guilty – not likely, given how enthusiastically he was looking forward to having a lengthy public trial.

All the psychiatric reports are available together with transcripts of the expert evidence provided during the trial. The reports, to me, are of surprising length and detail – doubtless reflecting practice in the criminal courts of Norway, where experts are not subject to cross-examination on matters not covered in their written reports. The reports are also tediously repetitive, with observation and opinion often mixed up together. On the positive side, they provide a clear picture of each and every interaction between the accused and the doctors.

During the trial, much time was spent discussing the diagnosis of schizophrenia. This discussion was framed in terms of the criteria for that disorder described both in the American Psychiatric Association's *Diagnostic and Statistical Manual* (DSM-V) and the World Health Organization's *International Classification of Diseases* (ICD-10). The mental-health experts originally chosen by the court concluded that the killer was psychotic because he met the criteria for schizophrenia set out in both DSM-V and ICD-10. (It used to be possible to direct the court's attention to the warning in the introduction to the *DSM* that the manual was not appropriate for use in legal cases – a caution that no longer appears in newer editions. Expert witnesses are thus left with the choice of either explaining that there is no conflict between their opinion and the text of the *DSM*, or explaining why there *is* a real or apparent discrepancy.)

Tørrissen and Aspaas disagreed with the first assessment, stating that the killer was *not* schizophrenic and, moreover, suffered no serious mental disorder, psychotic or otherwise. The trial focused on the question of schizophrenia, largely ignoring other possible psychotic states. By far the most important of these largely unexamined possibilities was the presence of a paranoid psychosis, possibly in the form of a delusional disorder.

Deciding whether or not an accused person has a psychotic illness is usually relatively straightforward. Typically, there is a history of contact with mental-health services before the offence. The Utøya killer's only mental-health records were from his childhood, and could not contribute much to the question of whether or not he was now psychotic. The clinical skills of a psychiatrist lie largely in recognising when the patient's account, however odd it may appear, does not amount to psychosis. This is particularly important for those of us who work with offenders. It is not uncommon, for example, to encounter offenders who report being troubled by hearing voices, or that they experience persecution from various sources. Occasionally these are the product of a psychotic illness, but most commonly they reflect the struggle of a vulnerable and damaged person to cope with the very real threats in their environment. In short, not all people who report hearing voices and believe they are being persecuted are psychotic. Psychiatry is more about avoiding the false attribution of madness than the exercise of some superfine insight that divines madness in what to the uninitiated would seem to be normal.

(In my experience, offenders rarely pretend to be mad in the hope of avoiding conviction or to improve the conditions of their detention. The occasional person who does, rarely manages a convincing performance. I remember trying to persuade a man awaiting trial for drug trafficking that shaving off the hair on the left side of his head and his beard on the right side, while sitting naked in his cell repeatedly claiming to be the reincarnation of the Hindu god Shiva, just wasn't going to run either as a basis for a defence of insanity or as an indication of his unfitness to plead.)

A number of features are considered characteristic of schizophrenic disorders. Not all of them need to be present, but at least some must be observable to support such a diagnosis. Hearing hallucinated voices is the most common symptom, present in more than 70 per cent of cases. Delusion, in various forms, is probably the next most commonly recognised state of mental disturbance. One experience reported by many sufferers is that of discerning personal messages hidden in media such as newspapers, radio or TV; another is that external agencies influence or control a person's thoughts; yet another is the sense that a patient's innermost thoughts are somehow available to others.

Relatively common but subtle disturbances occur in a patient's capacity to react emotionally in an appropriate manner, with the range of their potential emotional responses becoming limited – or, as it is sometimes termed, "flattened". Occasionally there are disturbances in the use of language, often referred to as "thought disorder", though obviously only utterances are observable, not the cognitive processes themselves. Rarely observed by today's psychiatrists are disturbances in intended movements, the so-called "catatonic" features, though in my opinion they are not uncommon if you know how to look.

In addition to the symptoms mentioned above, there are characteristic ways in which a schizophrenic illness may develop. The disorder can come on over a matter of days or weeks with clear and dramatic changes in the patient's state of mind and behaviour. Alternatively there can be insidious onset, in which psychotic features gradually emerge over months or even years. (Usually, a more rapid onset of symptoms is associated with a quicker and more complete recovery.) In almost all cases there is an obvious difference between how the person was before the illness and how they are while ill.

The case could be made for a substantial change having occurred in the Utøya killer during the five years preceding the massacre – from sociable and ambitious to reclusive and fixated on computer games and extreme right-wing ideas. There were, however, continuities: he remained ambitious and boastful, seeking to be seen not just as a celebrity but as a powerful leader. What changed was the context in which he pursued these goals. In isolation, his political ideology became more and more extreme. This can happen to people who lose contact with the moderating influence of other members of a political party seeking power within the limitations placed on effective political action in a democracy. The killer continued to seek admiration and influence, at first through interactions in one of the internet's fantasy worlds, and subsequently through a fantasy of leadership in a movement of his own imagining. These changes are not of a kind observed in the early stages of a schizophrenic process, but they are still compatible with the development of such a condition.

Husby and Sørheim pointed to other changes in the man over these years. They note the development in him of an excessive fear of infection and contamination, and comment on his escalating preoccupations with his appearance, which he apparently came to believe was deteriorating to such an extent that he needed both plastic surgery and cosmetic dentistry. He began, according to his mother's evidence, to eat strictly alone, as well as wearing a face mask around the house to protect against germs and possibly to hide his imagined disfigurement. In his interview with Tørrissen and Aspaas, the killer acknowledged becoming increasingly fearful of catching some infection in the weeks and months leading up to the attacks. He admitted that he had consulted his general practitioner about wearing a face mask around the house.

The reason he gave for increased vigilance against infection was his need to remain in peak physical condition for the coming attacks. In a similar vein, he connected the idea of obtaining further plastic surgery (he had already had a nose job) with his need to look his best for what he believed would be his upcoming martyrdom. Tørrissen and Aspaas took the view that this explanation made his actions less likely to be indicative of psychopathology.

Husby and Sørheim considered that the killer's compendium showed evidence of schizophrenic thought disorder, and that this abnormality was also apparent in the language he used in their interview. They placed particular emphasis on the use of neologisms – specifically, those neologisms coined by psychotic individuals, in particular those with schizophrenic illnesses, which do not refer to any clearly defined object or state of affairs. One term that Husby and Sørheim pointed to was *national Darwinism*. Even if the killer had coined it, it would not have been the type of neologism found in schizophrenia, because he gave a lengthy definition that, though it may not have been convincing, was comprehensible. (In any case, this was not a new phrase but one he had borrowed from the writings of the right-wing polemicist Michael Scheuer.) Other examples of supposed neologisms were equally unconvincing as indicators of the presence of a schizophrenic language disorder.

One important matter at issue was whether or not he was deluded about the Knights Templar. The experts did not base their views on what was written in the compendium alone, but on his responses to their enquiries about the existence of the organisation, and whether or not he was some kind of great leader in this order. The answers he gave to the first two doctors who had examined him were different from those he provided to the second set of experts. He led the first doctors (who were examining his motivations for the massacre) to conclude that he was acting on behalf of the Knights Templar, an organisation that (he asserted) actually existed in the modern world. In the second series of interviews – which occurred in the context of his wish to challenge the previous psychiatrists' opinions that he suffered from a schizophrenic illness – he claimed only to look forward to the emergence of such an organisation.

For the Utøya killer, what had been at stake with the first two psychiatrists was his desire to promote his image as a powerful, heroic resistance leader. In the second round of examinations, with the new set of experts, what was at stake was taking centre-stage to expound his political views before the media. Had the opinions of the first two psychiatrists prevailed, the trial would have been reduced to a brief affair in which he would have been found psychotic and in which no witnesses would have needed to be called other than these experts. There would have been no opportunity for him to make any statements from the witness box or the dock.

Husby and Sørheim concluded that the killer "believes he knows the thoughts of others ... this phenomenon is considered to be psychotically based", i.e. implying a schizophrenic disorder. The doctors are careful to report that the man said, precisely: "I know what other people are thinking; I don't guess, I just know." At another point, he described how, as a salesman, he became confident in his ability to divine the intentions and desires of potential customers. In my opinion, these features are suggestive more of an exaggerated belief in his ability to read others (in the everyday sense), rather than a psychotic experience of being able to directly read the content of another person's mind. More convincing was the psychiatrists' suggestion that the killer experienced newspapers, radio, television and the internet as broadcasting coded messages especially for him. Their evidence for this may be reinforced or undermined by the man's ambiguous response to an enquiry into why he believed this. He said he could not elaborate on the matter, and "unfortunately I have already said too much". At another point, however, he denied these communications were aimed specifically at him.

Both sets of experts noted that the killer maintained a poker face throughout the interviews, with no obvious expressions of emotion, which Husby and Sørheim interpreted as a sign of "flattening", found in some people with a schizophrenic illness. The doctors also considered that he was unable to recognise, let alone describe, his own inner emotional state and therefore had alexithymia, a technical term I had thought long defunct, which refers to a total lack of insight into one's own feelings. Tørrissen and Aspaas enquired of the killer about his rigid, inexpressive face and elicited the response that he chose to keep his feelings to himself, adding that this was a discipline aimed at not giving his interrogators any advantage in the quest to break him down. Tørrissen and Aspaas took the view that his notions of being spied on could be attributed to understandable caution and a realistic concern about being detected while building bombs and preparing for the assault.

Tørrissen and Aspaas proposed that the killer might be suffering from *pseudologia fantastica*, as opposed to delusion. This condition, first described by the psychiatrist Anton Delbrük in the nineteenth century, is known to French psychiatry by the delightful term of *mythomanie*, and in the English-speaking world by the rather more prosaic *pathological lying*. In my opinion, the description of *pseudologia fantastica* in the older psychiatric texts does indeed potentially capture many of the elements in the man's ideas and behaviour related to the Knights Templar. The central feature of this condition is an extensive and elaborate fabrication that is not primarily about deceiving others about matters of fact, but about creating a new and false identity for yourself. The 'pseudologues' become caught up in their own self-aggrandising fabrications, which, in large part, they come to believe. This condition is about self-deception on a grand scale as the person forsakes reality and finishes up performing on a stage of their own imagining.

Importantly, the pseudologue usually behaves in a manner that would have been appropriate if the fabrications were true. In forensic practice, we usually encounter these people after they have been charged with fraud and deception. They differ from the usual run of con artists by persisting in their deceptions long after they are to their benefit, continuing even when they have created a situation certain to lead to their exposure. Many years ago, one of my patients, caught up in his performance as an aristocrat, purchased a top-of-the-line Jaguar, paying with useless cheques. He could easily have escaped and converted the luxury automobile into cash at any number of less-than-scrupulous second-hand dealers. 'His Lordship' not only kept the vehicle, but also returned to the same dealer a few months later to have his first, free, servicing.

Tørrissen and Aspaas consider *pseudologia fantastica* to be the product of abnormal personality development unrelated to a psychotic process. In this they are in agreement with many who have written about the condition, including myself. However, when pathological liars are caught up in their complex fantasies, their degree of self-deception makes it very difficult to distinguish them from patients in the grip of delusion. Some of the great German psychiatrists of the late nineteenth century, such as Emil Kraeplin and Richard Krafft-Ebing, would diagnose such people as having paranoid (delusional) disorders.

Pseudologues can raise real problems for criminal courts. To be able to give evidence or be tried for a crime, you must be fit to take an oath. How can someone tell the truth if they are unable to distinguish fact from fantasy? The issue came to the fore for me in a trial in which a key witness was a police informant who himself had been diagnosed as having *pseudologia fantastica*. My role was to express an opinion as to whether or not he was able to keep his oath to tell the truth. In the end, the judge took the view that *any* witness promising to tell the truth may or may not be capable of fulfilling that oath. He therefore allowed this witness to proceed, but the jury was advised to treat the witness's testimony with appropriate caution. (Ironically, a year or so later, when the witness himself was facing charges of fraud and deception, the court took the view that he was unfit to plead, and should be committed as a patient under the Mental Health Act. He finished up in my unit for treatment.)

Husby and Sørheim perhaps tried too hard to fit the Utøya killer into the box labelled *schizophrenia*. They might have been wiser to try the box labelled *delusional disorder*, though that would have created its own problems. Tørrissen and Aspaas were, perhaps, a little overeager to normalise what the killer had said about his beliefs and experiences, particularly around the Knights Templar. Both pairs of doctors were under considerable pressure, and it is proper to be cautious in making any criticism. In my view, all the experts tried to be professional and focus on the mental-health issues. They explicitly attempted to ignore the political and social contexts, both as they applied to the actions of the killer and in the context within which they were now being asked to operate.

The killer's defence amounted to justifiable homicide. He contended that he was a combatant fighting on behalf of true Norwegians against those who would destroy their nation and its core identity. No such defence exists in common law jurisdictions, and I doubt there is any real basis for such a defence in these circumstances in Norwegian law. The inquisitorial process does, however, give far greater latitude to judges on what they will allow in their courts.

It could be argued that a precedent was set when Norwegians who had collaborated with the Nazis and the Quisling government during the Second World War defended themselves on the basis that they believed they were acting in the best interests of Norway. In my view, though we know that the Utøya killer saw himself in much the same situation, it was somewhat eccentric of the court to accept any parallel with a mass murderer acting to further his own idiosyncratic beliefs. Furthermore, the court received expert testimony that, at the very least, he was probably a case of *pseudologia fantastica*, even if not actually deluded. I would have thought the combination of these factors granted the judges ample opportunity to prevent him from having the opportunity to prance and preach before journalists from around the globe.

The killer was not driven by ideology, but by his need for admiration, power and fame. He left the Progressive Party because it did not promote him as fast as he felt was his right: he did not leave for ideological reasons. He moved from "Andersnordic" of *World of Warcraft* into looney right-wing websites because he had failed to establish the fame among fellow gamers he felt was his right. He moved from right-wing conspiracy theories and martial fantasies to mass murder because it seemed his only road to personal vindication – and enduring fame. Ideology made up the content of his final self-presentation as a mass murderer, but the form was made up of the pursuit of fame and vindication, as it had been again and again in his previous engagements with the outside world.

There can be debate about whether or not the Utøya killer fulfilled the Norwegian legal system's criteria for full legal responsibility, and about whether or not he fit into the current definitions of any particular psychotic disorder. What is *not* debatable is that he was mentally disturbed, and what most people would probably label as mad. Grandiose, obsessional and obsessive, deeply resentful and ultimately murderous, he was subject to various psychopathologies that made this tragedy possible.

He had his weeks in court, and potential mass killers acquired another world-famous figure to emulate. A young German boy, on the anniversary of the Utøya massacre, shot and killed a number of adolescents in Munich before killing himself. He left behind several documents, among which were writings about his predecessor: for this particular young man, the Norwegian was an admired model whom he wished to copy.

CHAPTER 12

Ever after

M WAS AN intelligent, good-looking Melbourne man with many features that should have guaranteed him social and economic success. But he was destined to spend many years in prison, much of this term in maximum-security conditions.

At the age of nineteen, dressed in army fatigues and armed with an M14 carbine and two other rifles, M had walked the short distance from the home he shared with his mother to an area alongside Hoddle Street, a busy road, where he began shooting. He targeted drivers, cyclists and pedestrians, killing and injuring until two courageous police officers managed to reach him and bring the slaughter to an end. After his arrest he made a number of statements about having intended to die from police fire. He also said, "You're not laughing at me now, motherfuckers!" and "This is payback on everyone!" The victims included Georgina "Gina" Papaioannu (twenty-one), Dusan Flajnik (fifty-three) and John Muscat (twenty-six).

The judge at his trial said he was "responsible for one of the worst massacres in Australian history, as a result of which seven people died and nineteen were injured ... Many more were fortunate to escape death or injury due to the indiscriminate discharge of over a hundred rounds of ammunition from three weapons, at passing motorists, and then police, as they attempted to apprehend him." The judge noted the community's understandable horror and outrage, and said: "There was, and I think there still is, a sense of bewilderment as to why a highly intelligent, educated, young man with no previous criminal history could have done what you did."

To the extent the court attempted to answer the *why* of the massacre, it relied first on mental-health experts' reports suggesting that M had a fragile, disturbed personality and was, at the time, under a number of stresses that had overwhelmed him; and second, on the ease with which powerful weapons could easily be acquired.

In infancy, M was adopted, joining two other adopted children in what appeared to be, at the time, a stable and reasonably prosperous family. His new father was an officer in the Army, and his new mother had abandoned her own career to look after the children and home. Families of career soldiers may be internally and emotionally stable, but they are almost always geographically unstable, owing to moves from base to base and periods of parental absence on postings where the family cannot follow. Perhaps such pressures led to the parents separating when M was twelve years of age. He remained with his mother, but regular contact with his father continued.

His early school years do not seem to have been marred by any difficulties fitting in and socialising with other children, unlike so many future perpetrators of massacres. On the contrary, he seems to have been bright and outgoing at primary school and in the early years of his secondary schooling. The problems came later – not in the form of his becoming withdrawn, but in his adopting an increasingly superior and dismissive attitude to his one-time friends and classmates. The source of this change appears to have been his belief that he had outgrown his peers and reached a far greater level of maturity. This conceit was based on his decision that his future was to be an officer in the Australian army, like his father, and he had put away childish things to focus on this goal.

His sense of being more mature was reinforced by what he believed was his greater success with girls, a belief for which there may have been some grounds. He certainly claimed to have had sexual intercourse with a student teacher when he was only fourteen, and was disbelieving when I suggested that, if that were true, in my opinion he had been the victim of sexual abuse, which might have added to his later problems. Whatever the validity of my suggestion, what is true is that, in addition to having prematurely adopted the persona of an adult soldier, he came to regard himself as more than usually sexually attractive. His self-image came to be tied to these two identities.

M's expectations appeared to be realised when, by the age of eighteen, he had become an officer cadet at the military academy in Canberra and had an apparently devoted girlfriend. Then it all fell apart. I was never clear about how it happened, but in a matter of months M was dismissed from the academy and the Army because of problems arising from undisciplined behaviour. In his view, he had been subjected to a gross injustice, in that his account of events had been rejected in favour of an opposing one given by an NCO who had a grudge against him.

The pillar on which he had erected his dreams for the future was destroyed. The father whom he so admired, he said, failed to come to his aid. He was back living with his mother, despairing, angry, harbouring an intense grievance. He had only his girlfriend to turn to, and she was soon lost to him too. A life in ruins; where to turn next?

How M ended up committing a massacre was considered at his trial. There was general agreement among the expert witnesses that, at the time, he had been depressed at least to some degree, and suicidal. The assumption that this was an impulsive act in a disturbed and intoxicated young man went largely unchallenged. The choice to go out and massacre people who were strangers was explained by the judge as a function of M being caught up in fantasies of death and glory from long-term exposure to violent media, in particular the movie *Rambo*. This view was supported by M's having worn combat fatigues for the killings.

My long-term involvement with M did not start until five years after the massacre. Initially, my role was to report regularly to the prison authorities and the parole board on his progress. I was able to interview him repeatedly over the next twenty or so years, as he grew older and changed, growing out of some difficulties and into new ones.

In our initial meetings, M's account of the events leading up to the massacre differed from those suggested by him to the police at the time or presented later in court. This new narrative must be considered in the light of events after his sentencing and imprisonment. The media had compared him to mass killers in the US, such as the University of Texas shooter. Prison officers and fellow prisoners alike also accused him of being just such a perpetrator. I suspect M accepted this label if for no other reason than that being an evil genius who had planned and executed a plot to commit a massacre was an identity preferable to the alternative: being a disturbed, distressed youth who, having failed to make it as a soldier and been rejected by his girlfriend, got drunk and went out shooting people at random. When I first encountered him, he certainly did possess an encyclopaedic knowledge of lone-gunmen massacres, which he spoke about with enthusiasm and at length. Central to the new narrative was planning and intent, rather than an impulsive act of grievance-fuelled violence.

Either story could fit the known facts. The problem for M was that embracing the persona of a gunman working to a plan would make even more remote the chances of progressing out of maximum security to medium security – and then on to minimum security and even to possible release on licence. M was an intelligent man, and was well aware of this. Why, then, flaunt this new identity? In part, because at that time the possibility of release seemed too unlikely to matter. In my view, more important was his tendency to grandiosity, which had characterised him as an adolescent and still as a prisoner. In time, he would realise his error and attempt to change how he understood the massacre, and how others viewed his role in those events – in particular those who controlled his prison placements and chances of release.

I often visited M in his prison cell rather than the usual venue of the medical centre. He kept his cell immaculate. His books and other possessions were carefully organised and placed, as far as was practical, with perfect symmetry, the tallest volumes at the centre of the shelf. Though he always seemed pleased to see me, and always remained polite, his level of agitation would sometimes increase as the visit progressed. I discovered that the source of this distress was quite simply my incorrigible untidiness. My papers always tend to migrate from desks and chairs to the floor. Such objects as pens, notebooks and folders, in my presence, take on lives of their own, dedicated to escape. I also have a bad habit of putting my feet up whenever there is any suitable or unsuitable surface within reach.

As a result, this young man would be reduced to scrabbling around on the floor collecting stray pages and wandering pens, which he tried to return to something approximating symmetrical order. He would always apologise while engaged in tidying me up but, as he admitted, he just could not stop himself. This performance became a ritual part of our interactions, which we both tried to pass off as humorous. On the few occasions that I asked him to stop he would comply, but his anxiety would rapidly build up to a point where it became too painful for either of us to tolerate.

This need to exert rigid control over his surroundings led to repeated conflict with fellow prisoners and prison staff. The disputes with staff often centred on what he saw as their failure to adhere correctly to prison regulations. He became not just a barrack-room lawyer but a real expert on the laws governing prison management, and every aspect of human-rights legislation potentially applicable to a prisoner. As the years went by, he moved from official complaints to initiating legal proceedings against various departments of the prison and justice bureaucracy.

At one point he seemed to spend as much time in court arguing his case as behind prison walls. He would occasionally win, but win or lose, he received considerable attention from the media. In some ways, his taking on the prison system for failing in its responsibilities or duty of care was admirable, but it was not to his long-term advantage. If he were ever to be moved out of a high-security to a medium-security facility, let alone have the remotest chance of parole, he needed to keep a low profile. His best hope of eventual release depended on being forgotten by the public and politicians. He persisted out of principle, but also, in my opinion, because he enjoyed the litigation process. Whatever damage he suffered, he welcomed his moments in the spotlight and, even more ruinously, in the pages of the popular press.

I don't believe it made any sense for the authorities to allow these battles – almost always about trivial matters – to escalate to full-scale court cases. Not only did they often lose in court, they spent vast amounts of public money on legal fees. Common sense is not part of being a rigid and obsessive person; nor, unfortunately, does it often manifest in bureaucracy personnel. To both the obsessive and the bureaucrat, it is the *principle* of the thing that matters, not the pragmatics. Nothing is too trivial or too petty *not* to require a principled stand.

The result, for M, was that whatever small chance he may ever have had for release evaporated. The result, for the correctional services, was being exposed repeatedly as petty and vindictive.

CHAPTER 13

Disrupting the script

The media

Most eventual massacre perpetrators share common objectives and motivations, and often acknowledge in their writings and postings the influence of previous lone mass killings. Even when they make no such admission, their internet and reading histories tend to reveal a preoccupation with their antecedents.

Ideology has often been a part of the puzzle of lone mass killings long before the emergence of killers who overtly declare their connection to terrorist movements. Three of the lone mass killers I assessed subscribed to extreme right-wing ideologies, though they made no claim that their actions were in furtherance of those ideas. Earlier lone-actor mass murderers sometimes left behind manifestos and justifications that cited, for example, Nietzsche, proclaimed imagined military affiliations or referenced Nazi ideas (such as the Columbine killers did).

Today, claiming terrorist justifications seems to have replaced purely ideological justifications, though the themes of persecution, a sense of personal superiority, military fantasies and 'striking back' remain unchanged. What has facilitated this change, I suspect, is the influence of the internet, with its pseudo-communities of extremists who all share the belief that they represent a persecuted elite.

The mass media do not create the psychological and social conditions productive of lone mass killers, but they do publicise a script that gives shape to the plans, actions and justifications of vulnerable men who are already susceptible. In particular, the media provide the fame these killers crave, and the publicity for their claimed justifications. Inadvertently, by making known the details of the attacks, they potentially offer models to be followed. The emergence and spread of the lethal use of cars, vans and trucks provides a clear example.

The influence of detailed media reports on the Columbine massacre illustrates the shaping of subsequent school and university campus shooters. To take a few examples among many: in May 2018, a seventeen-year-old boy who committed a massacre in Santa Fe, Texas referred, in a mobile-phone video before the attack, to both the Columbine massacre: "I'm going to be the next school shooter in 2018. [...] When you see me on the news, you'll all know who I am." This young man dressed to go out killing in clothes modelled on those of the Columbine murderers, even down to wearing a similar badge and T-shirt. He also selected the same weaponry used at Columbine. His inspiration came from multiple websites devoted to school shootings, and from Columbine reports in particular. His stated to goal was "to kill at least twenty people" – a reference to the 2012 Sandy Hook killings. The websites, many of which idealise mass killers, give details of the words, clothes and weapons. Such detailing acts to perpetuate the fame of previous mass killers. The Sandy Hook killer himself was discovered, after the massacre, to have extensive knowledge of media reports on the Columbine murders. He used that massacre as a template for his own attack. The Virginia Tech killer wrote that he would be a martyr like the Columbine killers. A man who killed nine people at a community college in 2015 in Roseburg, Oregon (including Rebecka Ann Carnes [eighteen], Kim Saltmarsh Dietz [fifty-nine] and Lucero Alcaraz [nineteen]) had written: "Seems the more people you kill the more you're in the limelight," and "Spill enough blood, the whole world knows who you are."

In an excellent article in *The New York Times* on what the writer terms "school shooting copycat syndrome", the mother of one of the Columbine killers is quoted as saying, "We don't do this intentionally, but we glorify shooters by showing the damage they have done ... all the crying, all the empty seats ... and people's rage, this has a particular appeal for them."

Once upon a time, all except the privileged elite derived their social status from a restricted number of their fellows. Their audience was among those they knew: family, neighbours, workmates, fellow professionals and members of the same organisations and clubs. Today, media outlets make it possible for us to perform before an audience of strangers, and to be the audience for strangers. The distinguished forensic psychiatrist Park Dietz was one of the first to point out that media coverage was central to the spread of lone mass killings: "The predictably high publicity attending these crimes is among the motives of their perpetrators."

What people see on television and read in news reports affects their behaviour. The most striking example is the reporting of suicide: a number of studies point to the fact that media reports of suicide, particularly by celebrities, induce a copycat effect that increases the rate of attempted and successful suicide in the subsequent days and weeks. In the past, this had been termed the "Werther effect" after Goethe's romantic hero, who killed himself for love. The publication (in 1774) and ensuing popularity of his novel, *The Sorrows of Young Werther*, were blamed at the time for increasing youth suicide. A copycat effect of international proportions can follow the suicides of famous people (e.g. Kurt Cobain in 1994); this now well-accepted pattern has led media organisations in many Western countries to adopt codes of conduct covering when and how such deaths should be reported.

Lone-actor massacres are far less common than suicide, making impossible the type of large-scale studies that established the association between mass media and suicide. One analysis led by the psychiatrist Christopher H. Cantor of the impact of media in seven

Australasian mass-homicide cases found clear evidence in at least four of them that they had been directly influenced by one or more of the preceding massacres. The study examined the time relationship between attacks in the West and found a pattern: a widely publicised lone mass killing would be followed by a number of actual or attempted imitations over the next few months. These were followed in turn by a period of relative peace before another well-publicised mass shooting triggered a further bout of similar killings. (In the US, the frequency of massacres is now so high that it is almost impossible to discern such fluctuations in what has become a continuous flow of such tragedies.)

Simply placing sensible limits around the detailed reporting of lone-perpetrator massacres is far more difficult than doing so for suicides. The massacres are newsworthy because they are shocking – not only because of the loss of life, but also because it is so easy to imagine oneself falling victim to such a killer. There is nothing the casualties could have done to change their fates; next time it might be *you* in the wrong place at the wrong time. (A report in the *Guardian* claimed that 7 per cent of Americans have been at, or near the site of, a lone mass killing at the time it occurred.)

Another element that tends to bring home the widespread relevance of these events is the sense that the atrocities are attacks on all of society, and that we are all in some sense a target for the killer. In reporting on the victims, the media rightly present a picture of random destruction. When they report on the perpetrator, they conjure up an image of an awful destroyer, either mad or evil. If media portrayals of these events attract imitators, then the image the copycats are seeking to reproduce is just that: a destroyer as terrible as he is evil. The lone-actor massacre is the embodiment of a shameful, utterly wicked criminality.

(Psychiatrist and philosopher Karl Jaspers warned, at the end of the Second World War, of the danger of demonising Hitler and the Nazis. He feared that yielding to notions of *evil* and *monstrousness* in describing and explaining their dreadful acts would guarantee that our culture would forever be haunted by their memory and, above all, their iconography. Jaspers understood the appeal to the abject and resentful of appearing as a powerful monster. The lone mass killer eagerly embraces such a public persona.)

As we shall see below, a 1996 government initiative affecting gun ownership following the Port Arthur massacre proved to be a significant factor in reducing the occurrences of lone mass killings in Australia. However, another factor was the way the killer came to be viewed. After the initial, predictable portrayal in the media of him as a demonic, psychopathic figure, journalists began reporting on the details of his *real* qualities as a dim, friendless, weak, inept and craven man whom no one in their right mind would wish to emulate. The dramatic decrease in the frequency of lone mass killings in Australia may well have had as much to do with responsible media practice as with new gun legislation and schemes.

Making changes to the way reporters and established media outlets deal with accounts of mass killings is difficult enough; but exercising any influence over what appears on the internet presents challenges of greater magnitude. Forget about dreams: the internet is increasingly the royal road, if not to the unconscious, certainly to the recesses of the human mind. Personal revelation, attempts at public presentations, revealing ramblings and obscure expositions jostle for the surfer's attention. Hits are affirmations online. As one deluded patient eagerly informed me, his website – filled with recriminations and accusations against a supposed Masonic child-molesting cabal – had received over 400 hits, so there had to be some truth to his suspicions.

Lone mass killers attain their moments in the limelight, and those who murder enough people can claim enduring fame online. The University of Texas killer currently generates over 3 million citations in a Google search; the Port Arthur killer, over 50 million. Sites devoted to mass killers are now so numerous, they constitute a separate category of the internet. Whatever else they reveal, a number of them certainly paint a vivid picture of what draws some, at least, of our fellow citizens to the lone-killer script. One example from a web page that openly declared itself as being in praise of "mass-shooters" contained the following:

> Even my brain cannot fully grasp the courageousness of these heroes. To stand up to an ENTIRE society and stick to your beliefs and make the ultimate sacrifice is an act of TOTAL heroism. They should be given medals of honour.

The hero fighting and dying alone, one against the rest, is an image that might be marred by reason when recalling that those who die are unarmed men, women and children going about their lives and presenting no conceivable threat to the destroyer. But that misses the point. Those who admire and become mass killers experience themselves as having been repeatedly damaged to the point where their own lives are not worth living. *If I am the centre and measure of the world, if my self-actualisation and the realisation of my potential is the point and purpose of existence, then those who have obstructed, denied and rejected me on my path to individual salvation have destroyed the only good that exists in my world.*

Everyone now knows it is possible to go out and commit a massacre. The models for how to carry through such a dreadful action are available to us all. In December 2016 in Berlin, a man drove into pedestrians attending a Christmas market, killing twelve. A few months earlier, eighty-seven pedestrians had been killed in a similar manner in Nice. In January 2017, an angry, psychotic young man, possibly under the influence of amphetamines, went on a rampage in Melbourne. He had spoken earlier about imitating the attacks in Germany and France, strongly suggesting a copycat influence. He drove into the city centre and entered a shopping mall at high speed, mowing down pedestrians, injuring many and killing six, including an infant in a pram.

Subsequently, in Melbourne, three additional incidents have occurred in rapid succession of men attempting to kill multiple people by driving their cars into crowds. It is difficult not to think that these attacks were anything other than contagion. Similar attempts between 2017 and 2025 to inflict multiple casualties using vehicles have occurred in New York, London (UK), Toronto, Tokyo, London, Ontario (Canada), Guangzhou, New Orleans, Munich, Magdeburg (Germany) ... and on it goes.

The media, in my view, are central to any strategy to reduce the frequency of lone mass killings. Clearly, such attacks should be reported; the only question is about the manner in which media outlets do so. There is an awareness among some media circles and scholars of the need to alter the way in which lone-actor massacres are reported in order to make them less attractive to anyone already receptive to the notion of imitating such behaviour.

Ari Schulman, an American journalist and editor of the magazine *The New Atlantis*, made the point succinctly in 2013 when he wrote: "To discourage mass shootings, more needs to be done to deprive the killer of an audience. Never publish a shooter's propaganda, hide their names and faces, minimise the specifics and gory details." German psychiatrist Tanja Neuner and colleagues emphasise that in order to prevent people from identifying with massacre perpetrators, media coverage of mass shootings should avoid not only glorification but also demonisation.

The Australian academics Glynn Greensmith and Lelia Green have suggested that coverage of mass shootings in the media should withhold details of the perpetrators' names and images, as well as limiting the amount of information about their methods. They further recommend avoiding speculation about killers' possible motives, and in particular refraining from publishing any manifestos or rants put out by murderers before their attacks. The importance of such a disruption in the lone mass killer's script is as apparent as are the difficulties in applying such a policy.

The focus of reports on such events, according to Greensmith and Green, should be on the victims, not on the killer (as I have done throughout this book). I would add that doing so helps to emphasise the cowardly nature of such attacks on defenceless people, and the pathetic state of an individual whose response to their own failures is to destroy others along with themselves.

There is another way in which the media may encourage the imitation of such violent behaviour. There is a tendency in the aftermath of a mass killing to lower the threshold for reporting on events even vaguely related to the original tragedy, magnifying the impact and drama attached to the original attack and attacker. For example, in the wake of the Sandy Hook shootings, reports ranged from guns being found on school premises to the suicide of a college professor in his office. One of the reasons that datasets such as those collected by the New York Police Department have so many incidents in which there are no fatalities (and sometimes no injuries) is the influence of the spate of reporting of vaguely similar events following a major mass shooting. By refraining from coverage that, at other times, would not earn such prominence, the media could help reduce the hype surrounding a massacre, so attractive to potential imitators.

Limiting the coverage of certain types of crimes to prevent copycat offences has long been a policy in the UK with regard to attacks and intrusions on the British Royal Family. (The practice developed following eight assassination attempts on Queen Victoria, many of which were imitations of earlier attacks.) The Royal Family continues to attract inappropriate behaviour, such as people forcing their way through secure cordons or attempting to break into palaces or even launch violent attacks. The vast majority of these intruders or would-be assailants are mentally disturbed, and after being contained by the Metropolitan Police's Protection Command, they are managed in a manner that will most likely prevent a recurrence of the behaviour. The priority in almost all cases is psychiatric treatment. Those apprehended are only very occasionally charged with offences: everything is done to avoid publicising the incident, discouraging copycat incidents.

When I was involved with a group of colleagues carrying out research into attacks on the Royal Family, we discovered documents covering previous attempts to harm royals, including details of a

1981 assassination attempt in New Zealand: a young man had shot at Queen Elizabeth. The man had been captured rapidly and disarmed. Later the same day, he was certified under the mental health act and transferred to a secure psychiatric unit. No publicity whatsoever was given to these events. I realised I had been present on the day, not far from where the event took place; even more remarkable to me was that I remained in total ignorance of what had occurred, as did all but a very small number of officers protecting the Queen. Quite probably Her Majesty had also remained in ignorance of the event. (I was, at the time, the director of psychiatric services for the region in which the attempted assassination had occurred. In theory, the man could not have been committed and transferred without my knowledge – though, obviously, he had been.) There was no publicity, and no copycat incidents occurred: no one who might have been liable to imitate the attack ever learned about it.

In stark contrast were the events surrounding a man who successfully gained access to a royal birthday party at Windsor Castle in 2003. This man, an obscure comedian, dressed in a strange confection of Arab dress, announced himself as Usama bin Laden and kissed Prince William twice on the cheeks as a stunt. The man's photo and name appeared on the front pages of a number of daily newspapers, and the event was reported in some detail on television. Over the next few weeks, there were over twenty attempts to break into royal palaces, or gatecrash events at which royals were present: would-be intruders sometimes even dressed in an approximation of Arab garb, as had the comedian. The offenders were a mixture of drunks, the mentally disordered and the plain silly. These copycat events were kept out of the media.

These two vignettes hopefully make clear the advantages of not publicising events that might provoke imitation, as well as the price of giving publicity to such events.

What stands in the way of change? In the US, any attempts to limit press freedom have been likely to face opposition on the grounds that doing so would be unconstitutional. It is worth recalling, however, that it was in the US that the first attempts to develop guidelines on the reporting of suicides were developed and introduced.

There would be less of a problem if it were only reckless journalists and audience-hungry media outlets that stood in the way of responsible reporting. The promotion of reporting that neither demonises nor confers celebrity on the perpetrators is one thing; it is quite another to prevent politicians or law-enforcement agencies from using these tragedies – however inadvertently – to increase their power and influence. Public fear and outrage generate waves that can be ridden by agencies and individuals all the way to gaining greater influence, control and funding.

I am not for a moment suggesting there is a conspiracy to exaggerate the threat of lone mass killings to extend the reach of the state. Government agencies respond to the demands made upon them, and, reasonably enough, use what methods they can to ensure they have the funding to discharge their responsibilities. Lone mass killings are certainly used by politicians pushing for more effective gun-control legislation. The many thousands who die each year as a result of the enormous numbers of guns circulating in American society sadly have less impact on the public consciousness than the dozens who die in lone-actor shootings. Pragmatism has thus dictated the use of such incidents to try to reduce the far more numerous tragedies occurring every day in the homes of US citizens. (The death toll from lone mass killings pales into insignificance compared to gun deaths from accidents, suicides and domestic homicides.) Unfortunately, this strategy militates against pushing for a more low-key, strategic approach to the reporting of these events.

On the other side of the gun debate we have proponents of self-arming such as the National Rifle Association (NRA) using these massacres to *promote* gun ownership. Apparently, if students and good people everywhere were toting their newly purchased guns, a would-be mass shooter would himself be shot down in a hail of bullets before even getting started on his murderous project. *Kill, kill, kill – to stop the killing.* The NRA's message would appear to be more effective than the pleas of the gun-control advocates, to judge by the surge in gun purchases that occurs after a widely reported lone mass killing or terrorist attack in the US.

There is room for hope that, despite these countervailing forces, even in the US, the media may stop inadvertently promoting the behaviours they so vigorously condemn. Outside the US, where lone mass killings have not become so much of a political football, there are indications that the message is getting through about the dangers of the wrong kinds of reporting – that it increases the risks of imitation. (The same cannot currently be said with regard to lone-*terrorist* mass attacks.) The media took on board the evidence about their reporting of suicide, and acted effectively. That success is now taught to every journalism student as an example of responsible reporting. Irrational fear, blind belief and simple ignorance just occasionally give way before the evidence of the numbers.

Guns

One commonly expressed view holds that the solution to lone-actor massacres is tighter gun controls. If only it were that simple. There have even been suggestions that what made it possible for the lone-actor massacre to emerge at the beginning of the twentieth century at all was simply the availability of guns capable of rapidly inflicting multiple casualties.

The handguns used by Ernst Wagner in 1913 were of a type that had been available for many years. The collection of guns dragged up to the top of the University of Texas tower by the shooter in 1966 could almost all have been purchased in the US over several previous decades. On the other hand, such massacres did become a regular event, with ever-increasing casualty rates, in the US following the lifting of prohibitions on the sale of semi-automatic weapons. The use of these weapons increases the number of people likely to be killed and injured. But does it explain why lone-actor massacres have been occurring more frequently both in the US and around the rest of the Western world?

The claim is sometimes made that gun ownership has always been a central part of the American way of life. The available US gun ownership statistics are often contradictory, depending on the source. According to federal government figures, the number of households in which there are one or more guns has decreased over the past fifty years from about 50 per cent to closer to 30 per cent. The number of registered guns in the US, however, increased from about 6 million in the early 1990s to over 16 million in 2013. This apparent paradox reflects the fact that now over half of all guns in the hands of registered gun owners are owned by 3 per cent of the people. We have little idea how many unregistered guns are in circulation in the US but, given that hundreds of thousands are reported stolen each year, it is likely to be a substantial number.

Care must be taken when relating gun ownership to homicide of any type. The homicide rate has *decreased* in the US over the past forty years by some 50 per cent, from over eight fatalities per 100,000 population to between four and five. Despite this drop, the proportion of homicides that are gun-related in the US remains the highest in the Western world. Attributing the decrease in homicide to the beneficent influence of owning a gun would be so simplistic as to be silly; but it would be equally foolish to claim that guns explain entirely the US's historically high rates of homicide, let alone the rise and rise of lone-actor massacres.

Guns are not, for most of us, an inevitable part of a normal living environment. For their owners, they are often more than instruments for propelling bullets at high speed: they are objects of fascination, pride, a focus for fantasies and a central part of the owner's core identity. Handling, owning and firing guns, even just at shooting-range targets, can evoke fantasies of killing that may or may not be restricted to animals. (As a young man, I enjoyed shooting targets; I do not wish to recall whatever fantasies the rifles evoked in me at the time, but I cannot forget the excitement of being allowed, occasionally, to use military rifles and semi-automatics. These weapons were less accurate than the competition rifles, but were much more fun.)

The role of guns in mass shootings cannot be reduced to that of mere implements, as demonstrated repeatedly by the histories of so many lone mass killers. The shooters' relationship to their guns can be part of why they end up killing people.

Many of the murderers discussed in this book had a very special affinity with their firearms. The Dunblane killer spoke of his guns as though they were his children. Guns were one of the few areas in which the Port Arthur killer possessed any real knowledge, and of which he spoke with enthusiasm. For the Columbine killers, guns were a joint obsession. In one of my cases, lax gun laws were the reason the perpetrator of a massacre gave for having immigrated to Australia where, at the time, he could more fully indulge his passion for possessing and using high-powered weapons.

The earliest examples of lone mass killings involved perpetrators who had been in the armed forces and served with distinction; all had seen active service. Among the workplace shooters of the 1980s were, as we have seen, a number of Vietnam veterans. Since then, many shooters have harboured martial ambitions, and in some cases attempted to join the military – but few had actually managed to pursue a career in the services. For the last few decades, we have seen killers play-acting the role of soldier as they killed defenceless civilians. What has not changed is their pride in their guns, and their facility with weapons.

The response of the Australian community to the blow of the Port Arthur massacre is worth considering in more detail. There had been several lone-actor massacres in Australia and New Zealand in the decade or so preceding the event, and several had involved the use of semi-automatic rifles and had resulted in multiple victims. Between 1986 and 1996 over seventy people had been killed in such shootings. During this period, the rates at which mass shootings of this type were occurring was, on a population basis, significantly higher than in the US.

The laws governing gun ownership in Australia had largely been inherited from the laws of the UK, but over the years both the wording of the legislation and the degree of enforcement had tended to produce something closer the US model. What had not happened in Australia, though, was the growth of a powerful gun lobby; nor had there emerged the ideological defence of an individual's right to bear arms, let alone a constitutional amendment capable of making gun ownership a fundamental right.

Once the Australian media overcame their original shock-and-horror response to the terrible loss of life at Port Arthur in 1996, they began to ask how a man could acquire such a collection of automatic and semi-automatic rifles as well as other military hardware. Guns began to take centre-stage in the nation's need for an explanation of the tragedy and a solution to preventing any recurrence. The government at the time comprised a coalition of the Liberal Party and the National Country Party. These parties, by Australian standards, are to the right on the political spectrum. To its undying credit, this government, under the leadership of then-Prime Minister John Howard, promised Australians it would legislate to remove from the community the types of weapon used at Port Arthur.

This stance was not uniformly welcome within the ruling party, and was furiously denounced by a number of rifle and shooting organisations. There was no shortage of death threats directed at those who, in Parliament or the media, advocated gun control. I even received a modest collection of death threats myself, following a couple of TV interviews. The response of the great majority of the Australian population was, however, not just positive but enthusiastic about the goal of getting weapons of these types out of their communities.

Previous attempts to tighten handgun legislation had not been successful, and gun amnesties whereby citizens could hand in illegal weapons at the local police station with no questions asked had, for the most part, been ineffective. In 1996, however, legislation by the federal government combined strict new laws on gun ownership with a totally new approach to gun amnesty. Centres were set up across the country where guns could be surrendered. There would be no discussion of how the person came to own a particular piece of military hardware, and receipts were to be given and the assessed monetary value of the surrendered weapons would be provided to the donor. It was called a "gun buyback", not an amnesty – and that is exactly what it became. The other change was that in most states, it now became mandatory for anyone holding a gun licence to register every individual firearm they owned with the police.

Though strongly supportive of the legislation, I was sceptical about its success. On the first morning of the programme, I went to the gun buyback centre nearest to the hospital where I worked, in a leafy, prosperous Melbourne suburb far removed from the rural regions where hunting and shooting are still part of people's lives. Queues stretched around the block, of men carrying bags and dragging various containers; one was even pushing a supermarket trolley. These containers were full of very serious weaponry of all kinds. The gun buyback exceeded the government's expectations. They not only had to provide far more funds than had been originally budgeted, but also extend the time the centres were open.

Thirty years later, it is possible to judge the buyback as a success. There have been other lone-actor massacres since then, but none involving high-powered military weapons, and the numbers of dead and injured have been far lower than in the pre-legislation era. In the period 1986–96 the average loss of life from lone mass shootings was seven per year. In subsequent decades, there were only ten victims of mass shootings, an average of fewer than one every two years. The rate at which these events have occurred over the past thirty years has fallen well below that in the US, even correcting for population differences. Gun deaths have reduced from all causes: suicide, crime and accident.

There were other elements in Australia's response to the Port Arthur massacre that reinforced the effects of the buyback, such as an obvious cultural shift in attitudes. One of my neighbours, formerly a keen huntsman and shooter, owned a semi-automatic rifle alongside a small but impressive collection of sporting guns. Speaking to him during the buyback, I was not surprised that he had surrendered the semi-automatic – but I *was* surprised that he had removed all his guns from the family home, disposing of most and placing a couple at his gun club. He explained that the massacre had made him think again about having guns, however safely stored, in a home with growing children. He admitted that displaying his collection would no longer be a source of pleasure or pride. Though such reconsiderations were far from universal, that they occurred at all was indicative of an important transformation in society's approach to gun ownership.

The Australian solution would be difficult to apply in most other jurisdictions. Australia is an island, which makes strict control over the importation of weapons at least feasible. European nations usually have land borders with several other countries, and the European Union has reduced border controls that might prevent the importation of illegal weapons to almost nothing. Since the collapse of the Soviet Union, continental Europe has been swamped with military weapons from the old Soviet Bloc countries.

The US has land borders to the north and south. Currently the flow of guns across the border with Mexico is predominantly out of the US. If restrictive gun laws were introduced into the US, the direction of the flow would doubtless reverse. But the barriers to sane gun control are enmeshed in the politics of the Republican Party and bedevilled by the influence of the NRA on members of both Republican and Democratic Party legislators.

One of the barriers to monitoring the acquisition of guns, let alone ammunition, is that in many jurisdictions gun owners are licenced, but the guns they own are not registered. As a result, the whereabouts of guns in a community at any particular point in time become almost impossible to monitor, even if the initial purchaser of the weapon is known. One of the guns used by a lone mass killer I assessed had initially been sold privately years previously in another Australian state. It later entered the gun market, moving from state to state before eventually reaching the dealer who sold the weapon to this killer.

One solution to the difficulty of tracking weapons as they circulate in our communities is to not only licence gun owners, but to register all weapons and require that changes of ownership be officially recorded. In the case of motor vehicles, the driver is licenced, the car is registered and transfers of ownership are recorded: it does not seem unreasonable to require the same of people buying and selling firearms capable of killing people. This approach has been introduced in Canada as well as Australia. The Canadian law was introduced in 1989 following a mass killing by a man at Montreal's École Polytechnique, who, railing against the "feminists" he believed had ruined his life, shot and killed fourteen women selected at random (including Geneviève Bergeron [twenty-one], Barbara Klucznik-Widajewicz [thirty-one] and Maryse Laganière [twenty-five]).

In many Western cultures the script has developed with the gun at the centre. Yet guns are simply one type of instrument used to perpetrate massacres. They determine, to some degree, the potential extent of the killing. They are, to use the Aristotelian terms, the *efficient cause*, not the *final cause*. Lone mass killings are also perpetrated with blades, bludgeons and motor vehicles; there has to be a question over whether removing guns from the reach of those inclined to commit a massacre would eliminate the problem, or effect a bigger shift in the method of murder to these instruments. Gun controls are, therefore, part of the solution, not the whole answer.

Keeping them alive

Extraordinary as it might seem, one contribution to making the lone-actor script less attractive to many of the killers might be made by the introduction of a capture-not-kill policy whenever possible. As we saw at the start of this book, the British colonial administration in the Malay Peninsula had success in reducing the incidence of *amok* by capturing the *pengamuk* alive. As we have also seen, for so many of today's massacre perpetrators killing is a means to achieve certain goals that often include being killed or killing themselves. The massacre offers a way of committing suicide that is not a suicide, just as *amok* transformed the shameful and forbidden act of self-murder into a semblance of being killed in battle.

In considering the dramatic decrease in the number of lone mass killings in Australia after 1996, one emergent factor is the number of perpetrators who survived. In the US, up to 70 per cent of those who commit a massacre die among their victims, killing themselves or being killed by police. In Australia, nearly 70 per cent *survive* to face trial.

Sometime after the massacre in Aramoana, I spoke with a number of senior police officers, emphasising that keeping mass killers alive would be preferable so as to reduce their attractiveness to potential imitators. They listened politely, making no comment. Some months later, a local man began firing on passers-by from his home. When the police arrived in force, he rushed out, firing at them and yelling, "Kill me, you bastards!" He was brought down with a bullet through his thigh, and subsequently disarmed and arrested. Speaking the following day with a senior officer, I expressed my admiration for the restraint of his men. He stared at me before saying: "The fool missed, and will be having remedial training at the range for some time to come." That officer was, of course, correct: when someone is shooting at you and your colleagues, you are *obliged* to aim for the easiest target to bring them down most effectively, which is the chest.

Overpowering a man with a club or an axe is one thing; taking down a shooter armed with a rapid-fire rifle or handgun is quite another. Nevertheless, some massacre perpetrators do survive when law-enforcement officers negotiate or force their surrender instead of shooting them down. The murderous driver in the 2018 Toronto van massacre was taken alive by a policeman who resisted repeated provocations to shoot. (A video exists of this remarkable incident.)

The policy in most Western anti-terrorist agencies is to subdue offenders rather than kill them, whenever the former is compatible with the safety of the community and the agents themselves. This protocol reflects the importance of gaining as much information as possible from captured terrorists to aid in rounding up other members of the group before they can strike again. Extensive training is provided to police units that could be called upon to deal with massacre perpetrators as well, emphasising the potential value of taking the lone mass killer alive.

CHAPTER 14

The lone male

IN AN EARLIER draft of this book, I was asked why I had not discussed the role of masculinity as a cause of lone mass killings. My initial excuse? I was so used to men being, far and away, the most frequent perpetrators of *all* violent offending that the gender discrepancy seemed unremarkable. A brief consideration of the numbers, however, made nonsense of this response. Yes, men are overrepresented as violent offenders of many forms, including homicide. In some US datasets, men make up to 80 or even 90 per cent of homicide perpetrators. But in lone-actor massacres, they form a significantly greater proportion: upwards of 98 per cent of lone mass killers are male.

Masculinity and changing gender roles may be relevant in two ways: first is the extent to which these mass killings caricature the fantasy of the alpha male's death-and-glory last stand. Second is the resentment – amounting to hatred – of women, particularly their perceived emancipation from male dominance. This theme is clearly expressed in many lone mass killers' manifestos and postings.

The term *toxic masculinity*, in my opinion, too easily becomes a useful term for men to distance themselves from the problems created by the current construction of masculinity in *all* its forms. The problem is not 'toxic' masculinity; it is the current construction of masculinity in general that needs to be challenged. (Looking back on my own past, I regret the extent to which I exploited women in my personal and professional lives as a teacher and lover, wearing the guise of paternalism.)

Prevailing notions about the nature of masculinity and gender roles have deep roots in human history. Over time, there have occurred adjustments in what could broadly be termed 'female emancipation', though all too often these changes benefited only women in the upper social and economic classes. Similarly, the accepted and expected expressions of masculinity have altered to some extent.

Religion has been a major influence in setting and maintaining gender roles and masculine ideals. The Abrahamic religions, for example – Judaism, Christianity and Islam – developed within a cultural context in which male dominance and assertive masculinity were core qualities. In a world of struggle, scarcity and the constant threat of war, of high infant mortality and of relatively rigid hierarchies, where social position was determined by the father's status, any doubts about female fidelity could pose a threat to the prevailing power structure. Such values, enshrined in religious texts, are now increasingly at odds with social realities. Attempts by some religious institutions to adjust their teachings to modern mores have had limited success – but that very success has engendered a fundamentalist reaction, reasserting traditional roles.

Yet the challenges to classical masculinity probably have little relevance to most lone mass killers. On the contrary, the problem for many of them is frustration at their inability to attain the hallmarks of traditional masculinity to which they aspire. Failed soldiers, failed alphas, failures even in standing up for themselves: these are the preoccupations of the men who commit massacres, steeped in resentment and an accompanying sense of victimisation. Only in fantasy can they attain the rampant masculinity they desire. Ultimately, it is in their final death-performance that they aim to have their manliness recognised and admired.

Massacres are generally gun crimes, making it unlikely that the mass-murder gender discrepancy is a matter of men being more aggressive or having greater facility with violence, let alone being bigger or stronger. Based on the cases I have worked on and in the literature, most perpetrators of lone mass killings are not, in the main, more aggressive; they do not have histories of violent offending, or of being involved in physical conflict. They do usually have both a facility and fascination with guns, but are, for the most part, pushovers who flee from confrontation, much less violent interactions. They may have brutal fantasies and play violent video games, but by and large they avoid even contact sports or the rough-and-tumble of normal adolescent life.

The rise in the frequency of lone-actor massacres in the West has overlapped with changes in the social relationships between men and women. It is tempting, therefore, to try and correlate the two – but, as ever, correlation is not causation. Another temptation to relate lone mass killings to the changing role of women can be attributed to the fact that among these killers, some have specifically blamed rejection by women and female dominance for their actions. Incel killings stand out in this regard.

Yet women's progress towards any form of equality has been slow and partial. Men's privileges and positions have not been eroded by the increase of women in the workforce, for example. What *has* happened is that employers since the 1940s have hired a far larger proportion of the population by coopting women in addition to men into the workplace. Women are usually paid significantly less than men doing equivalent jobs; whatever the perception of some men that there are more women in senior roles, it is in fact only a fraction of what it would be if the mythical 'level playing field' existed. The wonder is that men do not feel more fortunate that their dominance in the workforce persists.

While lone mass killers, in their writings, may decry women's supposedly unfair advantages in the workplace and in wider society, their bitterest complaints usually focus on the sexual domain. Incel killers have expressed this directly. Here, in my opinion, we are dealing not with an issue of perception, but of reality.

Over the last fifty years or so, women's progress towards equality has been modest; but in much of the West, at least among better-educated women, attitudes towards relationships, reproduction and sex have changed dramatically. Increasingly, among better-off women, there is a rejection of the idea that marriage and children should form the core of their existence, with jobs, leisure activities and material goods relegated to desirable addenda. The days of 'any man is better than none' are disappearing. The days of 'one man for life', however unsatisfactory he may be, are almost over. Many if not all women can support themselves economically, socially, emotionally and sexually without tying themselves to a long-term relationship with a man – which they may still choose to do for a variety of reasons, but that is much less a forced choice with no alternative, at least among women who *can* make such a choice. The very social groups into which most lone mass killers are born, and from which they are likely to aspire to find partners, are those most affected by changes to female aspirations with regard to relationships and sexual behaviour.

These shifts in women's attitudes potentially disadvantage males who are less socially capable, as well as those who demonstrate traits such as dependency and rigidity or a need for control. The former have problems *establishing* relationships, the latter in *maintaining* them; hence more rejected men. Indirect confirmation of this trend shows up in the literature on stalking, a behaviour that has long been recognised, though not by that name. Until relatively recently, stalking largely consisted of the pursuit and harassment of the famous, of those the stalkers wrongly believed loved them or would come to love them, and of people the stalkers wished to frighten and upset.

Over the last four decades, two relatively new forms of stalking have emerged, becoming the most common type of this behaviour and causing stalking in general to become a kind of victimisation affecting between 10 and 20 per cent of women. The first is stalking of women by socially incompetent males who have failed to establish a relationship; it usually is a matter of desperation as well as the expression of anger at past failures. The second type predominantly comprises men who have been rejected by partners with whom they had had an established and – they believed – permanent relationship. In both situations, it is almost always women choosing to turn down unappealing suitors or to eject unsatisfactory partners. The relevance to lone mass killers is that most have failed to establish any but the briefest emotional and sexual relationships, and blame society in general or women in particular for refusing to recognise their so-very-apparent merits. The incel community includes both the rejected and the ejected.

The lone mass killer's problems with both masculinity and women play into the complex web of influences that drive them. However, they share these difficulties with so many men that they can have little value as risk factors. At best, they may simply contribute to making the lone-actor massacre decisively a crime of men.

CHAPTER 15

Sounding the alarm

IS THERE EVER a situation when a threat to commit a massacre should be ignored? The answer is *no*. Sometimes such threats are disregarded because of a reluctance to get involved, or to inform on a friend or associate. Even more troubling is when they are dismissed in a therapeutic and professional relationship.

You might expect mental-health professionals to be reasonably adept at dealing with threats. After all, recognising and responding to threats of suicide is part of their core business. In my experience, however, many of my colleagues seem nonplussed when confronted either by threats of violence directed at them or threats indicating that the patient wishes to harm others. All too often, the threat is either ignored or evokes some vague admonition to the effect that such statements are unacceptable.

In some states in the US, when a threat to kill is made, there is an implied legal obligation on a therapist to inform the person threatened, or to inform the police. This so-called duty to warn grew out of litigation following the 1969 murder of Tatiana Tarasoff by a fellow student who had been stalking her. The killer had told his psychotherapist at the University of California at Berkeley's student-health service about his wish to kill Tarasoff. The therapist had, in fact, informed the campus police. They interviewed the young man –

and accepted his assurances that he would not continue to trouble the woman. In the litigation that followed the murder, the court held that a therapist did have a duty to warn of an intended harm revealed by a patient in a course of treatment.

Outside of a few US states, the duty to warn has never been more than a possible guide to action. The duty is usually interpreted to apply only when the patient or client expresses a threat to kill a named person, or someone whose identity is reasonably apparent to the therapist. The problem is that, for the most part, threats to kill when expressed in therapeutic encounters are *not* specific to particular individuals, unless it is the therapist who is actually the target. Examples of threats to commit a massacre that have been considered in this book so far usually involved statements of general intent rather than the revelation of specific plans. In most Western countries other than the US, there is no legal requirement to rescue others, even if you perceive them to be at risk of harm – which can be considered to apply to most people who have been made aware of a threat to kill. The situation of a health professional is somewhat different, as they may be considered to have a professional obligation when it comes to threats.

The problem, in most cases, has been the failure to recognise the potential seriousness of threats. Sometimes even the meaning of what was said or written has not been realised until after the event, as seen in various school shootings (e.g. Parkland, Florida, in 2018) and workplace attacks before which the perpetrator had spoken to friends about wanting to kill certain colleagues. These threats occurred in contexts such as bars or social gatherings, in which such statements were not taken seriously. Sometimes, as with the Dunblane killer's letter prior to the massacre, the implied threat is so obscure as to only acquire meaning in retrospect.

The biggest problem, however, is that in everyday life threats to kill may be made that are devoid of any actual commitment to harm anyone. For each attack, there are probably hundreds of unrelated threats of mass murder made by other people. My colleagues and I regularly encountered such cases in our community forensic service, particularly after a widely publicised lone massacre. How do you separate those who have indicated, however vaguely, an intention to perpetrate massacre, but who have absolutely no commitment to taking any such action from those who may well act upon their threats?

This is a classic problem in threat assessment. Some experts contend that lone-actor massacres are so rare that it will never be possible to identify those at risk without falsely identifying thousands of harmless people. Their argument is that lone mass killings only occur at a rate of fewer than one in a million per year, and that the best available risk assessments for violence correctly identify 70 per cent of likely offenders, with 30 per cent of the population falsely identified. If the violence rate is ten per hundred, there will be seven correct attributions to thirty false identifications. Consequently, with a rate of one in a million for every lone mass killer correctly identified, over 300,000 people will be misidentified as potential massacre perpetrators.

It is a fallacious argument, because *risk* assessment should not be muddled up with *threat* assessment. Risk assessment uses actuarial or research-derived correlations to estimate the long-term probability of violence occurring in a population in which the rate of violence is known. Threat assessment is about the likely consequences of a situation that seems to point to an imminent disaster. For example, an engineer requested to evaluate the risk of collapse in a commonly used design for a bridge will rely on the mass of statistics on similar bridges in comparable situations; the likely conclusion will be that the risk is so low as to be negligible. The same engineer called to assess the chances of this bridge, once built, collapsing following the discovery of a crack in a weight-bearing support will ignore the overall risk of such bridges collapsing, and focus on the threat presented here and now. It is the potential damage from someone threatening a massacre, or acting in a manner that raises concern about such an action, that preoccupies those attempting a threat assessment – not the risk presented by a randomly selected member of the community.

In evaluating the chances that someone might commit a massacre, we are always dealing with a situation in which something has come to light about the person in question that raises real anxiety. To date, we lack information about how frequently anyone indicating in some way that they may commit a massacre goes on to attempt to act on their threats. We are thus left with two potential ways forward. One approach is to compare the behaviour, psychological state and history of the person making the threat with those of people who have actually committed a massacre. The other is to examine the motive behind the threat and the degree of commitment to carrying it out.

There are differences between the psychological and social characteristics of most people who threaten and most of those who commit such attacks. The killers have almost always spent long periods fantasising about violent last stands and dying with glory. The threateners occasionally indulge in such flights of fantasy. The killers often research previous mass killings through searches on the internet, and in books. Such preoccupations are uncommon among threateners. Actual massacres have usually been carefully planned and meticulously prepared, to the point of acquiring the weapons and skills in their use. It is rare to find a history of plausible preparation among threateners.

The killers are mostly social isolates (offline, at least), who see themselves as victims of injustice and rejection, about which they harbour intense resentment. Threateners may have alienated family and friends, but they are not social isolates: they are difficult people. Though they might regard themselves as victims of a malevolent world, they hope for, if not demand, a change of situation. The killers are often rigid and obsessive, with tendencies to grandiosity, whereas threateners are more likely to be disorganised and vacillating individuals with poor self-esteem. Threateners, unlike most attackers, often have histories of self-harm, substance use and antisocial attitudes and behaviour. Ironically, these features mean that those who threaten are more likely than actual lone-actor killers to fall into the high- or medium-high-risk categories on most commonly used risk assessments for violence.

Threats express intentions, but their enactment depends on the individual's level of commitment. Commitment can be conveyed through the levels of preoccupation, plausibility, planning and preparation that accompany the threat. In everyday life, most threats to kill – including threats to inflict mass casualties – are an end in themselves, with no attendant commitment to act. Threats fall into a number of categories:

- *screamers* use them to express feelings or draw attention to distress;
- *shockers* use them as attempts to frighten others;
- *schemers* threaten in order to manipulate others;
- *shielders* make threats to persuade a potential aggressor to leave them alone on the assumption that they are more dangerous than they might appear.

But just occasionally, threats are just what they seem – warnings.

Most of the people who indicate that they are considering committing a massacre are attempting to draw attention to their current distress. They are waving a very large red flag that should be difficult to ignore. As with threats of suicide, there needs to be an exploration not just of the probability of acting on the implied threat, but also of the sources of the current distress and disturbance that have led to the threat. The threat and the threatener must always be taken seriously when assessed, however initially remote the possibility of their acting may seem, or however often they have made suicidal or homicidal threats in the past. A response that is dismissive or lacks appropriate concern amounts to a challenge to prove that the threat is serious, which can risk precipitating a suicidal or homicidal response. Failure to take threats seriously also ignores the underlying desperation to which they often give voice.

The motives of people who threaten to commit a massacre are usually obvious. The majority are distressed and disturbed; seeing no way out of their current state, they are driven to consider suicide.

Typically, they feel they have been failed by others who have not taken their despair seriously. One young man, frustrated and angered by a comment from his community nurse, expressed his emotions by phoning the consultant psychiatrist to threaten a massacre. This act created a minor panic, and resulted in an immediate referral for a forensic mental-health assessment. In his interview, it became clear that he had made the threat impulsively. He had never had any preoccupations with mass killing, had no access to weapons other than household knives and had made no plans to act on the threat.

Some threateners want revenge, as in the case of a young woman whose treatment was ended by her psychologist following a tantrum in which she trashed the office. She responded by writing a letter to him outlining her plans to commit a massacre, blaming his rejection; she also sent a copy to the local newspaper. She had absolutely no intention of acting on such a threat, and had made no preparations or even considered the implications of taking such action: it was a bad-tempered response intended to cause distress to the therapist.

In the week following the Columbine massacre, I received an urgent request for the immediate assessment of a schoolboy who had told a fellow pupil that he was going to bring a gun to school and kill even more people than at Columbine. The boy arrived at the clinic in an ambulance, escorted by two police officers. The parents arrived soon afterwards in their own car. I was confronted in the waiting room by a very sulky-looking young man and two tense officers of the law. It took some time to detach him from the anxious police, and even more from the agitated parents, in order to bring him into the consulting room. On entering, he flopped into a chair; in a voice loud enough to be heard in the reception area, he said he had nothing to say.

After enough time had been allowed to pass in silence, to accord due respect to his stated intention to remain mute, he relented. We soon established that he did not have a gun, that there were no guns in the parental home and that he had never even fired a gun. The closest he had come to a loaded gun was to the holstered handguns of the two police between whom he had been sat on the ride to the clinic. He had made no plans or preparations for perpetrating the threatened massacre. He readily acknowledged that his expressed intent to commit a massacre had no attendant commitment to action, and there was no way in practice for it to become a reality.

This young man was prone to daydreaming. He had a lively fantasy life, though it rarely extended to imagined acts of violence, and certainly not to heroic last stands involving the massacre of antagonists. Like most intelligent adolescents, he had contemplated suicide on occasion when angry or bored. He had no history suggestive of depressive episodes beyond the moodiness appropriate to his age group. There was a circle of friends with whom he felt he could share interests and occasional confidences. He reluctantly admitted that his childhood, far from being miserable or disadvantaged, had been quite good. His parents, he supposed, were loving and concerned, and better than most of his friends' parents. Even his younger sister was apparently OK. His activities at school involved participation in the drama group and playing in the orchestra.

He was in his final school year and was considered virtually certain to obtain the kind of marks that would guarantee his pick of universities and university courses. And there, it transpired, lay the problem. The parents were both the children of immigrants who had struggled to make their way in life. They were ambitious for their children. Their eldest son's prowess academically had fostered in the parents the desire to see him go to medical school, which was their idea of a gateway to financial and social success. The school appears to have shared similar ambitions for their more-than-able student; at least, this is how the young man saw the matter.

Some weeks earlier, there had been a series of rows at home after the young man had made it clear that he had no intention of studying medicine – or law, which was his parents' other preferred option. He informed them that he would study drama or nothing. His parents appear to have recruited the school in their efforts to persuade him that he would be squandering his abilities and opportunities by such a choice. The arguments apparently culminated in his father's angry vow not to support him financially at university if he did not pursue a 'sensible' course of study.

The idea of using a threat to commit a school shooting to emphasise his determination to have his own way occurred to him when he realised how much attention the massacre at the American school was garnering, not just in the media but among everyone he knew. He confided his supposed plan in the strictest confidence to a classmate who he believed, quite rightly, could be relied upon to spread the news to pupils and teachers alike. His expectation was that this would precipitate the kind of fuss that would provide ample opportunity to reaffirm his right to make a choice about his own future life. He did not expect the dramatic reaction that had in fact occurred, ending up with a police escort to a forensic psychiatric clinic, with both his parents and the school in a state of utter panic.

Here, as so often with threateners, the point was to produce an effect by the threat, not to carry out the promise implicit in it. Unscrambling the chaos generated by this young man's ill-judged provocation was not too difficult: sometimes the excessive confidence placed in the pronouncements of professionals such as myself has its benefits. In this case, all that was needed was for me to reassure the school with a statement to the effect that he presented absolutely no danger to anyone, and that this was a prank gone wrong. He agreed to spend an hour a week with a school counsellor, which seemed a modest price for the right to return, given how much disruption he had created. His parents, once reassured, were remarkably understanding. I heard later that he had successfully completed his final year. Like many children of prosperous people, he decided to take a gap year before proceeding to university. My guess is that he probably ended up following a course that at least approximated to his parents' hopes and expectations.

There is also a small group of what could be called *chronic* or *career threateners*. These people usually have histories of phoning police and emergency services to say they are about to commit some murderous or otherwise dangerous act. Not infrequently, they have histories of finishing up in emergency rooms following threats to kill themselves. They pop up among the group who make threats to kill prominent figures. In the aftermath of a widely publicised massacre, members of this group are likely to add threats to imitate the latest mass killer. They are often female, and are always seriously disturbed and distressed people who often form part of the marginalised and homeless in our supposedly caring society.

A number of these people have wound up in prison as a result of their threats. Some have been repeatedly admitted to psychiatric units, in which they rarely stay long. Equally rarely do they receive much in the way of subsequent treatment and support from the mental-health services. Assessing the level of risk these people present of committing a massacre is not a problem. Managing their social, interpersonal, psychological, psychiatric, physical and sometimes intellectual difficulties and deficits is the challenge.

Buried among the relatively straightforward cases of threateners are those in which the threat may indeed be a warning of a commitment to act. A man in his early thirties was referred after revealing to his university counsellor that he had been thinking about committing a massacre. There had been no recent publicity around mass shootings, but the previous year, a university in the same city had experienced a campus shooting in which staff and students had been killed and injured.

This man's presentation at the first assessment interview was unusual, to say the least. He entered my office dressed in army camouflage gear. He was soaked from the waist down, and water was dripping from his clothes and boots. He apologised for his state, which he explained had resulted from his fording a nearby creek. The explanation he offered for this eccentric behaviour was that he had taken a wrong turn on the way to my office, and had he simply retraced his steps he would have arrived late for his appointment. He therefore chose to take a direct route across the park through a relatively wide and rapidly flowing water hazard and so to my office. He expressed satisfaction that he had not kept me waiting by tardiness on his part.

He provided this explanation while standing to attention. He was only induced to sit down after my repeated assurances that the chair would come to no harm from a little damp. He was articulate and of good intelligence. He looked fit, which was not surprising given the daily exercise routines he later described in the interview. His manner was polite and deferential to a fault. He never failed to address me as "Professor". This level of formality is uncommon in Australia, and unknown among students.

He gave a history of having been an only child. His father was a construction worker who was often away from home for long periods working on civil engineering projects around the country. His mother, by his account, seems to have been a rather distant presence afflicted by frequent, extended periods of depression. At school he had a small circle of friends who shared his interest in the role-playing game *Dungeons & Dragons*. Academically, he was average or below average in most subjects except maths, in which he excelled. On completing schooling he had entered the Army, where he had spent the next ten years working largely in technical roles. He had never received a promotion beyond the rank of Private. He received an honourable discharge and then worked in the mines in outback Australia for some years before deciding to return to full-time education.

In the Army, he had kept a distance from communal life. He was a non-drinker, which probably excused him from much of the social life both in the military and in the outback mining towns. He had not maintained contact with any of his friends from school. His parents had died during his time in the military. He had had girlfriends, but none of the relationships lasted long, and even these brief encounters had ceased some years previously. He spent his leisure time playing computer games and reading. The books he favoured were non-fiction, with an emphasis on popular science and military history.

The way he presented his life story was in the form of a narrative dominated by accounts of repeated failures and frustrations. Interestingly, he blamed his own shortcomings for many of the difficulties, but there was also a fair amount of resentment directed at 'the system' and other individuals by whom he believed he had been mistreated. One failure that seemed to rankle more than the others was his inability while in the Army to obtain a transfer to a combat unit, and in particular to the SAS.

Obsessional features were prominent in his makeup, with multiple checking rituals and intrusive ruminations, both of which he would try to control or at least curtail with limited success. The compulsion to check had been a long-standing problem for him in work situations, because it led to slow, even if meticulous, performance. His rigidity and need for precise adherence to all procedures produced constant conflict with supervisors and coworkers. This in turn fed his resentment, because he always believed in his own mind that he was right to make sure things were done properly. He experienced attempts to persuade him to carry out tasks in a more expeditious manner as unjustified harassment stemming from the irresponsibility and stupidity of others. These problems not only led to confrontations, but also to repeated transfers or even dismissals.

For all his military bearing and impressive physical presentation, he was someone who found any form of conflict difficult to manage. It became clear in exploring his interpersonal difficulties that his habitual response to being confronted was to apologise, and though he obviously did not like admitting it, he usually ended up agreeing with whatever criticisms were being directed at him. He was a habitual sorry-sayer, which was doubly unfortunate given that his obsessiveness usually prevented him from changing the behaviour that had generated the complaint. Inside, however, he seethed with rage both at those to whom he found himself meekly submitting, and at himself for his weakness and inability to stand up against antagonists.

As so often with people who experience themselves as repeatedly making humiliating capitulations, he compensated through fantasies of aggressive self-assertion, ranging from reimagining conversations using superior verbal skills to humble his antagonist to violent retribution. He had also, from adolescence, indulged in detailed fantasies of taking violent revenge against those who had treated him with contempt. Included in these fantasies were often heroic last stands of the type described by many lone perpetrators of massacres. He even spoke of understanding people who had committed such atrocities, stopping short of actual sympathy.

He had a long history of bouts of mild to moderate depression, and had attempted suicide on two occasions – surviving the second attempt only by chance when he was discovered in time and transferred to hospital. There were no psychiatric assessments following these events, nor had he ever had any other contact with mental-health services.

At the time I saw him, he described feeling that he was being watched, and that people were laughing at him in the street or talking about him behind his back, particularly during lectures and seminars. The tendency to oversensitivity had been part of his way of being throughout his adult life, but had become much more troublesome in recent months in line with his deteriorating mood. He admitted that, once again, he had been contemplating suicide.

Through his Army career he had never been involved in actual combat, but he had acquired a high level of proficiency with weapons. He said he did not currently have access to a gun, but I believed him when he told me he knew where to obtain a semi-automatic rifle and ammunition. He was open about contemplating the acquisition of a weapon and committing a massacre on his university campus. He was well aware of the shooting at the nearby university the previous year, which he described as amateurish, poorly conceived and poorly executed – the implication being that his would be much more effective. He was equally open in admitting that he had told a therapist about committing a campus massacre in order to bring attention to the risk he presented. He even managed a degree of humour when he noted that the response from the therapist at least showed that she had bothered to listen. In my assessment interview, he had made no secret about his considering shooting people. When I suggested that this showed he wanted to be stopped, he said: “Of course I bloody do.”

You don't need psychiatric training and years of experience to understand that this man's threat needed to be taken seriously. He had the ability to perpetrate a massacre and some of the characteristics of those who commit such acts. He shared their history of radical loneliness, obsessiveness and rampant resentment. He was suicidal and he experienced himself as trapped in a situation where – as a result of his choices, such as changing his university programme – he could see no escape.

The literature on lone-actor massacres is full of suggestions about how potential shooters might be identified and prevented from progressing to their murderous attack. In practice, identifying individuals who demonstrate significant risk of launching into such acts presents serious problems. The literature that does propose ways of identifying potential shooters rarely considers in any detail what you can do if you manage to find someone potentially on the road to committing a massacre.

The obvious answer is to lock them up. To do this, we would usually have to ignore the constraints on illegal detention: as with the case being discussed here, such people may well not have committed any criminal offence. You could negate their civil rights by labelling them 'terrorist suspects'. But short of this, the law in most Western nations does not allow people to be arrested and incarcerated on the basis of their thoughts and fantasies. Making a threat to kill an individual or a member of a named group *is* an offence, but disclosing that you have had thoughts about murdering some unspecified group of people is not.

There are people that the current laws do allow to be deprived of their liberty not for what they've done, but what they might do. Those conspiring together to commit offences can be prosecuted for planning and preparing a crime. This does not apply to individuals, though such laws might possibly have been used against the Columbine killers and the San Bernardino shooters on the grounds that there were two people involved. Mental-health law has long been used to incarcerate individuals believed to present a danger of harming members of the community. The use of such powers has always depended on evidence of a mental disorder to justify their admission and treatment in psychiatric hospitals. In short, quite rightly, locking people up for how they think, or how they might possibly act in the future, is not made easy in a civilised society.

To return to our case: the man had not committed any criminal offence. Even if a magistrate could be persuaded to stretch a point and conclude that his utterances amounted to a threat to kill, this would have removed him from the streets for only a brief period, if at all. He did have a depressive disorder, and he had owned up to suicidal ruminations. I offered to organise his admission to hospital, but he was vehemently opposed to such a course of action. In theory, I could have arranged for him to be admitted as a compulsory patient under a section of our mental-health act. This would have necessitated overstating what I knew of the severity of his depression and of the risk of imminent self-harm. As readers will hopefully have gathered by now, I am not opposed to stretching rules for a good cause, or in what I regard, in my somewhat paternalistic way, as being in a patient's best interests. In this case, the gains from forcing him into a psychiatric unit were uncertain at best, and the potential losses in terms of losing his trust and willingness to cooperate were considerable. He had, after all, gone to some trouble to ensure that the risk he presented was recognised, and he was expressing the desire for help.

Forcing him into a hospital psychiatric unit would have destroyed any hope for a "therapeutic alliance", as we psychiatrists term the process in which patients do what we tell them to do. Had I imposed this on him, he could not have been admitted to any of the beds in my own hospital, because this was a maximum-security facility for mentally abnormal offenders; it did not accept patients on civil orders from the community. He would have been sent to an acute psychiatric unit under the care of a general psychiatrist. These units are busy wards in general hospitals with a rapid turnover of, in the main, acutely disturbed psychotic patients. The average length of stay is a little over a week. Even if the inpatient service was inclined to keep my patient longer, it is probable that his inevitable appeal to a mental-health tribunal would have gained his release. Furthermore, he was an intelligent man who, I suspect, if hospitalised, would have modified his story to suggest that his ideas about committing a massacre had been misunderstood, and had never involved any serious intention to kill.

The only beneficiary of committing this man, at this time, to a psychiatric institution would not have been him, or the community, but myself. The responsibility for any future disaster would have been shifted from me to others who would later sanction his discharge from hospital. Such are the temptations that need to be resisted when dealing with patients who may, just possibly, go on to do terrible acts.

The alternative to locking him up was to negotiate a plan of management, which would reduce the chances of a tragic outcome. The basis for such a plan already existed. He shared, at least for the present, the goal of finding the means to prevent him from committing a massacre. The first step was to establish his agreement to come to the clinic whenever he had an appointment. In many disorganised and distressed people, their agreement to attend a forensic clinic voluntarily often does not result in them actually turning up at the time of their appointment; however, this man's obsessive and rules-bound nature gave some reassurance that he would keep this commitment.

Before he left the clinic, I was able to introduce him to the clinical psychologist who would be providing most of the therapeutic inputs. She had considerable experience in managing threateners, and violent men in general. She was also someone whose personal and professional qualities usually resulted in her clients attending regularly and completing their programme of treatment. Convincing him that he should start a course of antidepressants was considerably more difficult: he had no problems swallowing vitamins and any number of natural remedies by the bottleful, but the very thought of consuming a product of Big Pharma was anathema.

In general, my attitude to such medication objectors is that it's their illness, and they are perfectly entitled to protect their disorder from the potentially disruptive effects of my prescriptions. In his case, there was a reasonable chance that the use of an appropriate antidepressant would shorten the duration of his current depressive symptoms, and it was thus worth engaging in the debate. The discussion usually goes down the road from *I won't take psychiatric drugs* to *they won't work anyway* on to *only in small doses, then* and finally to *all right, but I will blame you if they poison me*. How long it takes for the patient to reach this satisfactory conclusion, if they ever do, varies. So, as part of our deal about medication, I promised that although the university would have to suspend him until we agreed that the risk had passed, I would ensure his reinstatement.

This man's problems in life stemmed in no small part from his rigid, obsessive nature – which was also partly why his threat had to be taken seriously. But one benefit of managing such people is that when they say they will do something, they usually abide by it. Thus he did attend sessions regularly and, despite grumbling, did take his medication with almost religious adherence to timing and frequency of doses.

He made slow but gradual progress. His depression improved, and – somewhat to my surprise, and thanks to the university staff responsible for such decisions – I was eventually able to keep my promise, and he returned to his studies at the university.

I have described his case in some detail in order to illustrate the importance of taking a threat seriously, and the practical difficulties for intervening effectively when practitioners are faced with someone who presents a real risk of committing a massacre.

CHAPTER 16

Last words

As I hope I have made clear in this book, there are solutions to reducing lone-actor massacres. A range of actions could contribute to decreasing the frequency of these atrocities and decreasing the number of victims. To recap:

- We have noted how the media play a role in promoting copycat killings. We must also be practical: a massacre is always going to be – and deserves to be – newsworthy. Trying to restrain the messenger will not efface the message. Fortunately, responsible news networks have become cautious in reporting about the killers, instead gearing most of their reporting to the victims. What remains to be achieved is for the criminal justice system to follow suit and remove the opportunity for surviving killers to strut and pontificate before the global media. We should forbid trials from being additional platforms for them to parade their actions and ideologies before the public. (The trial of the Utøya murderer is an egregious example. The judge in the trial of the Toronto mass killer provides a stark and praiseworthy contrast. Justice Anne Malloy stated: "One of the issues I have struggled with is that the accused committed a horrific crime ... for the purpose of achieving fame. I refuse to actually name the accused.

I will refer to him as 'John Doe'. I will instead name the people he killed and injured." (Sadly, some media reports quoted her, yet went on to name the accused and tell of his ideas.)

- When killers survive, they should be packed away with as little fuss as possible into a prison or secure hospital, whichever is appropriate in the particular case. They should disappear as far as is possible from public view. This is for their own sakes as well as the affected communities; their only hope of moving on from a high-security prison to a less restrictive, medium-secure placement, let alone being given parole, is to be forgotten by the general public.

- Guns, for the most part, are the instrument of choice for lone mass killers, who have inappropriate and empowering relationships with their weapons. As I have stated, one useful barrier to the misuse of firearms would be to register all weapons and require that all changes of ownership be officially recorded – just as happens in most countries with regard to motor vehicles.

- Mental-health professionals should accept the link between psychotic disorders and increased violent behaviour of all types, and act upon their responsibility to manage this risk as part of good clinical care. However, as we have shown throughout this book, most lone mass killers do not have a diagnosable mental disease. If there is anything of value to be gained with what we have discussed, it is to shift the focus from specific mental disorders to a recognisable sets of personality traits and states of mind. Namely:

  — Rampant resentment or grievance
  — Rigid and obsessive characteristics
  — Withdrawal and social isolation
  — Despair and suicidal preoccupations

> — Grandiose pretensions to abilities not recognised by others
> — Fantasies of a suicidal, dramatic death
> — Fascination with guns and other weaponry
> — Fascination with previous lone-perpetrator massacres.
>
> When these and other potentially lethal personality traits are present, alarm bells should be ringing and actions should be proposed to prevent a potential massacre. The problem is that there are no people or organisations responsible for making the assessment and putting in place remedial action. It is as if we possessed a fire alarm without a fire department capable of putting out the blaze.

Two cases indicate how, even with clear indicators of impending violence, there was no one tasked with recognising the importance of the threats and responding to them effectively. The first was in April 2018. A young man, naked but for a jacket, entered a Waffle House franchise in Tennessee and opened fire with a semi-automatic, killing four people (including Taurean C. Sanderlin [twenty-nine] and Joe R. Perez [twenty]) and injuring two. The death toll would have been higher had a courageous man not risked his own life to wrench the gun from the shooter's hands. The killer had a history of mental illness of a schizophrenic type, and had been seen by local mental-health services. The previous year he had been apprehended by Secret Service agents while attempting to enter the White House, demanding to see the President. He also had a history of disturbed and threatening behaviour with a semi-automatic rifle.

His history did not suggest a predisposition to committing a massacre, but it should have raised a serious concern about violence. We know he was declared unfit to hold a gun licence, and his guns were removed. Despite this prohibition, his father is alleged to have given him the gun used in the attack. The massacre occurred because no mechanism was in place to monitor and manage this psychotic young man with such a high risk for future violence.

The second case is even more disturbing. In June 2018, a violent querulant entered the *Capital Gazette* newspaper office in Annapolis, Maryland, and opened fire on the journalists, killing five (including Rebecca Smith [thirty-four] and Wendi Winters [sixty-five]) and injuring two. He had been threatening the newspaper for several years, and the police had been informed. Instead of a mechanism to monitor and treat the threatener, the targeted victims, the editor and the journalists were burdened with the impossible task of managing their aggressor.

As indicated throughout this book, guidelines for assessing whether or not someone is a potential mass killer exist; what is lacking is an effective structure for undertaking such an assessment, and for taking action based upon it. Just as a fire alarm is linked to a fire department, a threat alarm should be linked to what I propose be termed a Threat Assessment and Response Centre (TARC), where:

- anyone (family, friends, work colleagues, fellow pupils, teachers, employers, mental-health professionals, law-enforcement officers, etc.) who fears that someone might be planning a mass killing can report their concern;
- all threat reports are filtered to weed out the frivolous and malign from the serious;
- serious threats are passed onto mental-health professionals for assessment and treatment, and/or police and other law-enforcement agencies for follow-up.

These centres would be modelled on a similar, existing structure, the Fixated Threat Assessment Centre (FTAC). In the UK, and later in Northern Europe and Australasia, FTACs are joint police and mental-health organisations. The original FTAC was set up in the UK to manage people who stalked, threatened or attempted to intrude on or attack members of the British Royal Family. The impetus for the unit came from a programme of research in which I was involved, that demonstrated the central role of psychotic illness in the majority of these offences. The problems originate in disturbed and deluded people, most of whom would have been given psychiatric treatment in the past, but are now out of contact with mental-health services.

The FTAC's function is to assess and manage the risk such people present, largely by ensuring they receive and continue to receive the treatment they need for their own sakes. The centre was evaluated as a dramatic success in reducing the rate of recurrence of problem behaviours. In most cases, it transformed a security problem into a mental-health problem.

Central to the effective functioning of the FTACs is the power, when deemed necessary, to access a subject's criminal and mental-health history as well as their internet search history and whether or not they have ever registered a firearm; FTACs can also have potential informants interviewed and premises searched, if required. Which of these powers are employed depends on the overall threat assessment.

Politicians who suffer similar problems with threateners, stalkers, unwanted intrusions and potential attackers came under the FTAC umbrella. Most relevant here was research that indicated the importance of mental disorders in lone terrorists. The FTAC's role was extended to the assessment and management of individuals identified by their behaviour to be at risk of progressing down to a lone-terrorist attack. (Its remit excludes members of terrorist organisations.) In Australia, people making threats to commit a massacre are also referred to the FTAC.

A TARC would function in much the same way, except the potential victims would not be royals, politicians and celebrities but the general public. Instead of focusing pre-emptively on assassins and specific targets, it would encompass lone killers considering random killings.

There exists a plethora of guides for the assessment of possible imminent violence in particular situations such as stalking, domestic conflict and threats in the workplace. These amount to a list of areas into which enquiries should be made, derived from factors that the literature suggests are associated with the progress to violence. The guidelines usually come together with training or written suggestions on how to interpret any findings. These threat-assessment approaches provide a template for the evaluation of someone who is raising concerns about their potential to become violent in the immediate future.

How, then, should one proceed with the assessment of people who draw attention to themselves through, for example, a combination of making threats, a telltale internet search history and the acquisition of the means to commit a massacre? It is clear from the many case histories which areas should ideally be included in any such enquiry. The first step is finding out, as much as possible, what is already known. This should include information such as:

- indications of social withdrawal;
- anything raising concern about suicidal tendencies;
- utterances about mass murder and terrorist outrages in a manner suggestive of approval or fascination;
- acquiring or possessing weapons that could be used in an attack;
- sharing fantasies relevant to possible attacks;
- threats to launch an attack;
- any history of past violent or threatening behaviours.

Documentation would need to be sought concerning the individual's criminal record and any police database dossier. Such efforts can be remarkably informative about contacts with law enforcement as a complainant, or as a person of interest, in situations that had not led to any convictions. Also of value would be any mental-health records, academic records and internet search histories.

The next step would consist of interviewing the individual to explore:

- what they see for their future: are they hopeful, pessimistic, despairing?
- whether or not they have become more isolated;

- whether or not they feel they have been deprived of their chance to succeed, or have been frustrated, ignored and actively impeded by others;
- their favourite films, websites, social media follows, computer games and books;
- whether or not they have harboured ambitions to enter the military or law enforcement;
- any possession of, or affinity with, guns and other weapons;
- their fantasy life;
- their political and social views;
- any history of suicidal behaviour and self-harm.

Attempts should also be made to explore their state of mind, including:

- mood, along with any thoughts of suicide;
- evidence for marked resentment based on memories of humiliations and rejections;
- any experiences of people talking about them in a derogatory manner, or ganging up against them;
- any thoughts about committing a massacre or other violent outrage.

A degree of scepticism would be understandable regarding the chances of anything useful emerging from interviews with someone dragged in on the suspicion that they might be contemplating a massacre. How much cooperation are you likely to receive from someone being interrogated on the basis of a casual remark or a misunderstood school essay? Equally, why should anyone who was in the process of considering or planning an attack expose themselves by answering questions from a police officer, let alone a mental-health professional?

In my experience with situations in which the possibility of a planned crime is at issue, you may well encounter furious resistance to participating in an interview. But just as often, you are met with a remarkable level of cooperation and frankness. In my practice, this most often arises in the case of sex offenders under supervision, when concerns are present about possible further offending. Those with nothing to hide, once their anger has settled, are usually eager to clear up any misunderstanding. Those who are indeed contemplating offending may decide that appearing to be fully cooperative is their best strategy. Once they start talking, even if it is to try to cover up the truth, there is always a chance of any sinister plan being revealed.

One morbidly jealous man, whose wife had fled in fear of her life to a women's refuge, agreed to see me to clear up the mistake. What eventually emerged was a detailed plan to kill her. I have little doubt he wished, at some level, to reveal his intention, and in so doing save both his wife and himself. Another perhaps more relevant situation involved a man seen by a colleague who had been apprehended in a government building at night, carrying a large knife. After being arrested, he claimed that he had just been curious, and was unsure as to the nature of the building. In a pre-sentence assessment for the magistrate's court, after being convicted of trespass and threatening behaviour, he revealed a long-term fixation on a particular politician who had an office there. He had planned to kill this man. He had been apprehended while seeking somewhere to hide until morning, when he could go looking for his victim. Fortunately, it soon became clear that he was deluded, enabling a recommendation for treatment. This outcome was in his best interests, as the fixation on this politician was ruining his life. It was also in the interests of the potential target: the offender was given effective treatment, and the threat was removed.

If someone is identified as a potential attacker, what then? The whole point is subsequent management. Much will depend on the individual's current level of commitment to progressing down a particular road. Two of the lone-actor mass murderers I have evaluated had doubts about carrying through their plan, right up to the last moment. One even claimed that, on the morning of the massacre, he had let the toss of a coin make the final decision. Had he had the opportunity to speak to someone when he was of two minds, a tragedy might have been averted.

Some potential offenders, when confronted by someone who is taking their threats seriously, find themselves forced to face the reality of their intentions. When they are challenged, plans that may have been driven by fantasies are now transformed into concrete choices – with consequences they may not wish to pursue.

What is to be done with someone whom investigators suspect may be planning an attack? Some readers may find it outrageous that the answer usually depends very much on how cooperative those under suspicion choose to be. Compelling or coercing compliance requires criminal law or, if there is an issue of serious mental disorder, mental-health law. But the law can be effective only if there are proper structures in place to apply it.

Imagine if the Virginia Tech killer had been identified as being at risk of committing mass murder by a TARC a week before the event. A search of his room would have uncovered the weapons, and searching his computer might have turned up a draft of his manifesto. The guns had been purchased without disclosure of his mental-health history, so in theory they could have been confiscated. Had he been persuaded to cooperate with a mental-health intervention, a long-term solution might have been possible. Without this cooperation, the progression to mass murder could have been averted, and he would have continued to be under constant surveillance.

There are other cases discussed in this book in which identification by a TARC would almost certainly have prevented tragedy. Had the Utøya killer been suspected – greater weight might have been placed on a report to Norwegian Customs that he had bought a quantity of explosive primer from an online shop in Poland – and his farm raided in the week or so before the attack, the discovery there of bombs, guns and his compendium could have sustained a criminal prosecution. Any psychiatric examination would probably have been far more enlightening, separated from the political pressures and the media frenzy that ensued after the tragedy.

I leave it to the courageous students of Parkland, Florida, and their comrades to bring some sanity to US gun laws. My role is to partner with mental-health and law-enforcement colleagues throughout the world to put in place TARCs and take responsibility for the identification and treatment of potential killers. These should be government-financed centres where mental-health professionals and law enforcement are linked in a joint effort. If such structures are created, the means are available to make them effective in spotting, treating and preventing some mass killings.

Bibliography

The following references are included for readers interested in pursuing particular topics discussed in this book, and as a tribute to colleagues whose works I have relied upon.

Barbosa, Duarte, *The Book of Duarte Barbosa: An Account of the Countries bordering on the Indian Ocean and their Inhabitants*, vols I and II, London: Hakluyt Society, 2010.

Barry-Walsh, J. *et al*, "Fixated Threat Assessment Centers: preventing harm and facilitating care in public figure threat cases and those thought to be at risk of lone-actor grievance-fueled violence", *CNS Spectrums*, vol. 25, no. 5, April 2020, pp. 1–8.

Bartos, Bradley, *et al*, "Controlling Gun Violence: Assessing the Impact of Australia's Gun Buyback Program Using a Synthetic Control Group Experiment", *Preventive Science*, vol. 21, no. 1, 2019.

Bates, L., *Men Who Hate Women*, London: Simon & Schuster, 2021.

Bennett, D. J. *et al*, "Schizophrenia disorders, substance abuse and prior offending in a sequential series of 435 homicides", *Acta Psychiatrica Scandinavica*, vol. 124, no. 3, June 2011, pp. 226–33.

Bernstein, M. A., *Bitter Carnival: Ressentiment and the Abject Hero* Princeton, NJ: Princeton University Press, 1992.

Blair, J. Pete and Schwieit, Katherine W., "A Study of Active Shooter Incidents in the United States, 2000–2013", Texas State University and Federal Bureau of Investigation, Washington, DC: US Department of Justice, 2014.

Cantor, C. H., Mullen, P. E. and Alpers, P., "Mass homicide: The civil massacre", *Journal of the American Academy of Psychiatry and the Law*, vol. 28, no. 1, 2000, pp. 55–63.

Chapman, S., P. Alpers, M. Jones, "Association between gun law reform and intentional firearm deaths in Australia 1979 to 2013", *JAMA: Journal of the American Medical Association*, vol. 316, no. 3, 2016, pp. 291–99.

Chester, G., *Berserk: Motiveless Random Massacres*, London: Michael O'Mara Books, 1993.

Cleckley, H., *The Mask of Sanity* St Louis: CV Mosby & Co., 1941.

Cook, James, *The Journals of Captain Cook*, ed. Philip Edwards, London: Penguin Classics, 1999.

Cullen, W. D., *Public Inquiry into the Shootings at Dunblane Primary School*, London: Stationery Office, 1996.

Douglas, K. S. *et al*, "Psychosis as a Risk Factor for Violence to Others: A Meta-Analysis", *Psychological Bulletin*, vol. 125, no. 5, September 2009, pp. 687–06.

Ellis, W. G., "The Amok of the Malays", *Journal of Mental Science*, vol. 39, 1 July 1893.

Fredholm, M., ed., *Understanding Lone Actor Terrorism: Past Experience, Future Outlook, and Response Strategies*, London: Routledge, 2016.

Gill, P., *Lone-Actor Terrorists: a Behavioural Analysis*, London: Routledge, 2015.

Gimlette, J. D., "Notes on a case of amok", *Journal of Tropical Medicine* 15, 1901, pp. 195–99.

Greensmith, G., "Reporting Mass Shootings" in *Ethical Reporting of Sensitive Topics*, London: Routledge, 2019.

Guapp, R., "*The scientific significance of the case of Ernst Wagner* and *The illness and death of the paranoid mass murderer, schoolmaster Wagner*: a case history" in *Themes and Variations in European Psychiatry: An Anthology*, eds S. R. Hirsch and M. Shepherd, Oxford: Butterworth-Heinemann, 1974.

Hampshire, S. *Innocence and Experience* London: Allen Lane Press, 1989.

Heok, Kua Ee, "Amok in nineteenth-century British Malaya", *History of Psychiatry*, vol. 2, no. 8, 1991, pp. 429–36.

Hunt, M., *The Mugging*, London: Secker & Warburg, 1973.

James, D. V., J. R. Meloy, P. E. Mullen *et al*, "Abnormal attentions towards the British Royal Family: factors associated with approach and escalation", *Journal of the American Academy of Psychiatry and Law*, vol. 38, no. 3, 2010, pp. 329–40.

Kelly, R. W. *Active Shooter: Recommendations and Analysis for Risk Mitigation, 2012 Edition*, New York: New York Police Department, 2012.

Langman, P., *School Shooters: Understanding High School, College, and Adult Perpetrators* Maryland: Rowman & Littlefield, 2015.

Lankford, A., "Public Mass Shooters and Firearms: A Cross-National Study of 171 Countries", *Violence and Victims*, vol. 31, no. 2, 2106, pp. 187–99.

Monahan, J. T., "The Individual Risk Assessment of Terrorism", *Psychology, Public Policy, and Law* (18), 2012, pp. 167–205.

Mullen, P. E., "The autogenic (self-generated) massacre", *Behavioral Sciences & the Law*, vol. 22, no. 3, 2004, pp. 311–23.

Mullen, P. E., "Pseudologia fantastica", in Gunn, J. and Taylor, P., *Forensic Psychiatry: Clinical, Legal and Ethical Issues*, London: Routledge, 2020.

Mullen, P. E., "Querulous behaviour: vexatious litigation, abnormally persistent complaining and petitioning", in *New Oxford Textbook of Psychiatry*, 2nd edn, eds Geddes, J. R., Andreasen, N. C. and Goodwin, G. M., Oxford: Oxford University Press, 2020.

Mullen, P. E. and Pathé, M., *Stalkers and Their Victims*, 2nd edn, Cambridge: Cambridge University Press, 2008.

Mullen, P. E., D. V. James, J. R. Meloy *et al*, "The fixated and the pursuit of public figures", *Journal of Forensic Psychiatry & Psychology*, vol. 20, no. 1, 2009, pp. 1–15.

Neiman, S., *Evil in Modern Thought: An Alternative History of Philosophy*, Princcton, NJ: Princeton University Press, 2002.

Neuner, T. *et al*, "Media running amok after school shooting in Winnenden, Germany!", *European Journal of Public Health*, vol. 19, no. 6, December 2009, pp. 578–79.

O'Brien, Bill, *Aramoana: Twenty-two Hours of Terror*, Auckland: Penguin Books, 1991.

Pathé, M. T., D. J. Haworth, T. Goodwin *et al*, "Establishing a joint agency response to the threat of lone-actor grievance-fuelled violence", *Journal of Forensic Psychiatry & Psychology*, vol. 29, no. 1, 2018, pp. 37–52.

Pathé, M. T. and Farnham, F. R., "Implementing multiagency strategies to prevent violent extremism", in Logan, P. *et al*, *Violent Extremism*, London: UCL Press, 2023.

Peterson, J. and Densley, J., *The Violence Project: How to Stop a Mass Shooting Epidemic*, New York: Abrams Press, 2021.

Rapa, L. J. *et al*, "School Shootings in the United States: 1997–2022", *Pediatrics*, vol. 153, no. 3, March 2024.

Schanda, H. *et al*, "Homicide and major mental disorders: A 25-year study", *Acta Psychiatrica Scandinavica*, vol. 110, no. 2, September 2004, pp. 98–07.

Scheler, M., *Ressentiment*, Wisconsin: Marquette University Press, 2019.

Seierstad, Å., *One of Us: The Story of Anders Breivik and the Massacre in Norway* tr. Sarah Death, London: Virago Press, 2015.

Taylor, P. and J. Gunn, "Violence and psychosis", *British Medical Journal*, vol. 289, no. 6443, 1984, pp. 1945–49.

Walker, N. and McCabe, S., *Crime and Insanity in England: The Historical Perspective*, Edinburgh: Edinburgh University Press, 1968.

Wallace, C., "Criminal Offending in Schizophrenia Over a 25-Year Period Marked by Deinstitutionalization and Increasing Prevalence of Comorbid Substance Use Disorders", *American Journal of Psychiatry*, vol. 161, no. 4, April 2004, pp. 716–27.

Warren, L. J., P. E. Mullen and T. E. McEwan, "Explicit threats of violence", in Meloy, J. R. and Hoffmann, J., eds, *International Handbook of Threats*, New York: Oxford University Press, 2014, pp. 18–38.

White, S. G., "Case study: The Isla Vista campus community mass murder", *Journal of Threat Assessment and Management*, vol. 4, no. 1, 2017, pp. 20–47.

Index